HARD SAYINGS OF JESUS
Embracing His Words of Life

Joel C. Seifert

NORTHWESTERN PUBLISHING HOUSE
Milwaukee, Wisconsin

Cover illustrations: Lars Justinen; GoodSalt, Inc.
Art Director: Karen Knutson
Design Team: Diane Cook, Pamela Dunn

All Scripture quotations, unless otherwise indicated, are taken from the HOLY BIBLE, NEW INTERNATIONAL VERSION®. NIV®. Copyright © 1973, 1978, 1984 by Biblica, Inc.™ Used by permission of Zondervan. All rights reserved worldwide.

All rights reserved. This publication may not be copied, photocopied, reproduced, translated, or converted to any electronic or machine-readable form in whole or in part, except for brief quotations, without prior written approval from the publisher.

Northwestern Publishing House
1250 N. 113th St., Milwaukee, WI 53226-3284
www.nph.net
© 2015 Northwestern Publishing House
Published 2015
Printed in the United States of America
ISBN 978-0-8100-2713-8
ISBN 978-0-8100-2714-5 (e-book)

Table of Contents

Introduction 5

One
Translations! Traditions! Troubles! 7

Two
"If You Don't Have a Sword . . . Buy One" 12

Three
"Blessed Are Those Who Mourn" 16

Four
"Out of Men's Hearts Comes Evil" 21

Five
"I Am Coming Back Soon" 25

Six
"If You Have Faith as Small as a Mustard Seed . . .
Nothing Will Be Impossible for You" 32

Seven
"No One Is Good—Except God Alone" 38

Eight
"Unless Your Righteousness Surpasses
That of the Teachers of the Law . . ." 44

Nine
"Unless You Hate Your Father and Mother . . ." 51

Ten
"Be as Shrewd as Snakes" 57

Eleven
Pearls Before Swine and Bread to Dogs 64

Twelve
"Why Have You Forsaken Me?" 70

Thirteen
"So They Won't Hear" 78

Postscript... 83

Introduction

John 3:16—*"God so loved the world that he gave his one and only Son, that whoever believes in him shall not perish but have eternal life."*

Matthew 11:28—*"Come to me, all you who are weary and burdened, and I will give you rest."*

John 11:25,26—*"I am the resurrection and the life. He who believes in me will live, even though he dies; and whoever lives and believes in me will never die."*

They called Jesus *teacher* during his earthly ministry. It's not hard to see why. As God's Son walked among us, his words did what the psalmist wrote about a millennium before: "The unfolding of your words gives light; it gives understanding to the simple" (Psalm 119:130). Jesus taught "as one who had authority." Long before telephone lines or cell phones could broadcast a message, Jesus' words gathered crowds by the thousands and the tens of thousands.

They still do. As you hold this book in your hand, I assume that you've come to know and believe in Jesus through his words or at least have been so intrigued by their message and power that you want to know more.

And perhaps you've found yourself running into a difficulty that's two thousand years old. Some of Jesus' words are hard. That's not what we might expect. God wants to communicate with us through the words of Christ. He speaks undeniable truth. And the sovereign Lord who designed the pathways of our minds and understanding knows well how to speak to us.

So why are Jesus' words so hard to understand at times? How can countless Christian denominations look at his words and disagree on what he's saying? Why can believers read the words of our loving Savior and wish he would have said something different? Different words of Jesus are difficult for us for different reasons. In this book, we'll consider Jesus' difficult words in three main groupings:

1. Sayings that are difficult for us to understand because of cultural differences or problematic translations
2. Sayings that we struggle with because they don't appear to be true
3. Sayings that we wouldn't expect from a loving God

This book is written for those who struggle with some of Jesus' words. I pray that includes you. His words are worth struggling with. At times we may need to grow in our understanding or leave behind our sins and portions of our worldviews, but in his word Jesus offers and gives us what he plainly says: *"Whoever believes in him shall not perish but have eternal life."*

Translations! Traditions! Troubles!

Matthew 5:32 (KJV)—*"I say unto you, That whosoever shall put away his wife, saving for the cause of fornication, causeth her to commit adultery: and whosoever shall marry her that is divorced committeth adultery."*

She holds the Bible in her hands, and it's hard not to hate Jesus, at least a little. Not long after getting married, she realized that her husband wasn't the man she thought he was. The caring and attentive man she dated was replaced by someone who was distant and cruel. She discovered that the time he spent on the computer late at night was used for looking at pornography. But through it all, she remembered the promise she made to God on their wedding day and the promises God made to her that he would use everything for her good. God could fix their marriage. God could make them stronger. Trusting in those promises, she was even willing to keep working on their marriage when she found out he had cheated on her with another woman. But he wasn't willing. After her years of committed effort, he divorced her.

She didn't resent Jesus for all of that. She understood that it wasn't God who failed in her marriage; her husband had failed. She could bear that pain. But Jesus' statement in Matthew chapter 5 seemed too cruel: "Whosoever shall marry her that is divorced committeth adultery." Her adulterous husband went on to have another relationship, but in those words it sounded like her Savior was punishing her. As faithful as she'd been, she would either have to live the rest of her life without the blessing of a husband or become an adulteress herself.

Poor Translations Can Make Jesus' Words Difficult to Hear

That's not what Jesus is really saying. Jesus likely spoke in Aramaic during his teaching and preaching ministry two thousand years ago. The accounts of his life and teachings (the four gospels: Matthew, Mark, Luke, and John) were written down in Greek. Jesus' words are just as true and relevant today, but we read them in translations. Many of those translations are very good and trustworthy, but none of them is perfect. And small errors in translation can lead to some very big problems.

Jesus' words in Scripture about divorce and remarriage are a good example of this. Perhaps you've come across these words before and wondered why Jesus seems to be punishing the "innocent party" in a divorce. Maybe you've heard churches or preachers saying that once someone is divorced, it's sinful for them to ever marry again (even if they were the ones who were abandoned). Maybe you've been in that situation and struggled with these words of Jesus too.

It's important to deal with what Jesus actually said. As strong a translation as the King James Version (KJV) is, it doesn't seem to handle this passage correctly. (The New International Version [NIV 1984 or 2011] doesn't do much better either.) When the KJV translates the verse as saying, "Whosoever shall marry her that is divorced *committeth adultery*," Jesus used a rare verb form that doesn't occur anywhere else in the New Testament. Based on a few similar verb forms—and a similar statement from the Old Testament book of Deuteronomy—a more accurate translation would seem to say that whoever marries a divorced woman "causes her to be seen as an adulteress."

Jesus' words in Matthew chapter 5 aren't punishing a woman who was left by her husband. Jesus is recognizing the terrible damage that can be done by an unfaithful spouse. To all onlookers, an unfaithful man may seem like a loving and faithful husband; they don't know that he has been untrue to his marriage promises. When he divorces his wife, the assumption that many would make is that she must have done something wrong. When she eventually gets remarried, they assume she'd been unfaithful to her first husband, possibly with this new man. Her first husband's loveless, selfish actions have "caused her to be seen as an adulteress." Jesus warns against that, not because he wants to keep the innocent party from another marriage but because he wants to protect them from that kind of slander and false judgment.

Over the centuries, how many people have struggled with these words of Jesus that seem so harsh and unkind? How many innocently divorced people have been told by church leaders or well-meaning Christian friends that they could never marry again? How many have held a Bible in their hands during one of the most difficult times in their lives and found themselves resenting Jesus, at least a little? Yet in those words Jesus wasn't laying another burden on that poor woman. He was there in his Word as the one who cares about that woman's reputation and now sympathizes with her in the challenge she faces. He wasn't forbidding the woman from remarrying; he was warning the husband about the full impact of his sinful actions.

Sometimes the struggles we have with Jesus' words aren't really with Jesus' words. Some of the struggles are with imperfect translations. That's why it's important to have faithful translations and well-trained clergy who can continue to study God's Word in the original languages so we can always make sure we hold to what Jesus really says.

Poor Traditions Can Make Jesus' Words Difficult to Understand

Matthew 19:24—*"Again I tell you, it is easier for a camel to go through the eye of a needle than for a rich man to enter the kingdom of God."*

The city of Jerusalem is surrounded by massive walls. To enter the city, you pass through one of the large main gates. Those gates are closed at night. Any travelers who come to the city at night need to enter through a different door, set low in the wall. This door is small, like the eye of a needle.

So the story goes. For at least five hundred years, Bible commentators and preachers have pointed to these "eye-of-a-needle" gates to help explain Jesus' comments in Matthew chapter 19. A camel could enter through such a gate, but it wouldn't be an easy process. The bags, treasures, and riches on his back would need to be unloaded. The camel would need to get down on his knees and make the difficult entrance. Do you see the comparison to a rich man? It's his riches that keep him from the kingdom of God. He can enter, but it won't be easy. He must unburden himself of his riches, get on his knees, and make the difficult entrance.

The eye-of-a-needle gates don't actually exist, however. There are some small gates in the city walls of Jerusalem, but those were built much later than Jesus' time. There is no indication in Scripture or in the historical record that any gates in the walls of Jerusalem were referred to as the eye of a needle.

Just like poor translations can cause unneeded struggles with Jesus' words, poor traditions can make it difficult to understand Jesus too. Over the years explanations and interpretations that often have no truth to them have been attached to passages. The "mark of Cain" (Genesis 4:15) has been explained as God giving the first murderer black skin. (The Hebrew text doesn't say that God put a mark on Cain but that he gave Cain a sign.) Jesus' response to Peter's confession of faith (Matthew 16:18) is interpreted as Jesus setting up Peter and his successors as earthly leaders of the church on earth. (Jesus says nothing about Peter's successors. His words are actually referring to Peter's beautiful confession that Jesus is the Son of God.) Traditionally, many have interpreted Jesus' words about the eye of a needle as him telling the rich to get rid of their wealth.

Take away that incorrect tradition about Jesus' words and what do you have? This time you have a saying of Jesus that actually gets *harder*. A camel can't pass through the eye of a needle. It's impossible. Does that mean that it's impossible for a rich man to enter heaven?

Jesus spoke these words to his disciples immediately after his conversation with a "rich young man." It's a touching and heartbreaking exchange. A young, wealthy man seemed earnestly to want to live a godly life. He strove to keep the commandments and thought—with no hint of self-glorification—that he truly had. Jesus looked at the young man and loved him (Mark 10:21) but realized that this man's heart wasn't as focused on God as the young man thought. When Jesus told the man to give away his wealth, this young man went away sad, finally realizing that he loved his money more than he loved God.

You can be rich and enter heaven. Scripture makes that clear. Abraham, David, Solomon, Job—Scripture is filled with examples of believers who had great wealth as a blessing from God. But you can't love money more than God and enter heaven. Love of earthly wealth is such a subtle sin that an earnest, God-seeking young man didn't even realize the hold it had on his heart. So Jesus speaks words of crushing law to reveal that sin—for the young man and for us. It's a hard saying, but not because it's so difficult to understand. It's hard because it brings a harsh warning for all of us.

Life in this world is messy and complicated. Divorce is difficult. Wealth can be deceitful. But Jesus speaks clear and honest truths. After clearing away the clutter of bad translations and incorrect traditions, may God grant us hearts to hear and follow his Word.

2. "If You Don't Have a Sword... Buy One"

Good things come to those who wait. *The pen is mightier than the sword. Look before you leap.* There's a reason those nuggets of wisdom have stood the test of time. They offer wise, practical advice. You'd do well to live by them.

But at the same time: *Time and tide wait for no man. Actions speak louder than words. Strike while the iron's hot.* These proverbs are just as true as the previous ones. But did you notice something? They give you the exact opposite counsel as the first set. They contradict one another. Trying to follow both sets is a recipe for confusion.

Contradictory advice is frustrating but natural. No human advice is perfect, and we know that advice like that is meant as a general guide, not an absolute rule. We (rightly!) have higher expectations of God's Word. So how should a believer react when it sounds like Jesus is contradicting himself?

Does Jesus Advocate Violence or Peace?

You can't find a better example of love and peace than Jesus. Believers have found strength in his call for us to turn the other cheek (Matthew 5:39). We recognize the truth of his words that "all who draw the sword will die by the sword" (Matthew 26:52). And Jesus didn't just speak words like that; he lived them. As he faced cruelty and injustice from the authorities of his day, he did not respond with violence. It might surprise us, then, to hear his words on the night he was arrested:

> Luke 22:35,36—*Then Jesus asked [the disciples], "When I sent you without purse, bag or sandals, did you lack anything?" "Nothing," they answered. He said to them, "But now if you have a purse, take it, and also a bag; and if you don't have a sword, sell your cloak and buy one."*

Roman soldiers were coming for Jesus. He would be arrested and killed. The disciples would face persecution. Is that why Jesus changed his view towards violence?

Actually, he didn't. Jesus wasn't advocating that the disciples arm themselves and try to kill the Roman soldiers. If you doubt that, just keep reading Luke's account of that night. As the mob appears to arrest Jesus, Peter draws his sword and attacks one of the men. Jesus puts an end to the violence (and even heals the wound of the man who came to arrest him!).

Jesus' view of violence didn't change. But he wanted his disciples to know that something else *did* change. When Jesus first sent the disciples out with the message of the kingdom of heaven, they found peace and acceptance almost everywhere they went. It was a blessed time for the spread of the gospel.

But as Jesus continued to preach, things changed. The leaders of the Jewish church realized that his message of God's free grace threatened their earthly power and authority. Now those spreading the gospel would often face earthly need and even violence.

We see that throughout history and even in present times. Christians face danger as they spread the gospel. The greatest news of love often is met with hatred. On a personal level too, we all risk difficulties in our relationships as we share God's Word. While Jesus isn't calling us to arm ourselves for the sake of the kingdom, he is calling us to expect difficulty and sacrifice as we follow him.

The next set of "contradictory" statements brings that out too:

Luke 9:59-62—*[Jesus] said to another man, "Follow me." But the man replied, "Lord, first let me go and bury my father." Jesus said to him, "Let the dead bury their own dead, but you go and proclaim the kingdom of God." Still another said, "I will follow you, Lord; but first let me go back and say good-by to my family." Jesus replied, "No one who puts his hand to the plow and looks back is fit for service in the kingdom of God."*

It doesn't seem fair. They heard Jesus' call, and they listened. They wanted to follow him. That's a good thing! And they weren't trying to procrastinate or shirk their duties. The men wanted to show respect to their family members by burying a dead father and bidding a family good-bye. And Jesus tells them they aren't fit for service in the kingdom of God. Isn't this the same God who calls us to honor our fathers and our mothers? the one who calls us to show love and respect for our family members? So how can he speak such hard, unloving words?

These words are hard, but they aren't unloving. In verse 57, this section begins with a man telling Jesus, "I will follow you wherever you go." That's a wonderful response of faith; God loves that reaction. But he also loves us and wants to prepare us for real faith and ministry. So he let them know: the only way to follow Jesus is to follow Jesus. He *has* to come first. If anything—our work, our hobbies, even our families—comes before Jesus, then he really isn't our Lord. He's just another thing in our lives. And he wants us to understand that so we don't set ourselves up for failure.

God has to come first. He wants that, because he knows that he's our only Savior. It's not out of love for his own glory; it's out of love for our souls. Does that mean that he comes before our family? Sometimes! The faithful husband who takes his children to church when his wife doesn't see the importance of it knows how difficult this truth is. The children who speak the truth to their parents about a sinful divorce know how hard this can be. The people who risk family conflict in order to give witness to the truth understand what "service in the kingdom of God" can cost us. But please understand: God's will isn't to separate us from our families. So often following Jesus will bring us closer to our families as we share devotion time together, as we honor our marriage vows, as we pray together and instruct one another. And yes, sometimes it will come at a cost. But even at those times, that cost will be felt because we're trying to show those we love what God's Word truly says. Even when following Jesus comes at a cost, he isn't calling us to dishonor our parents or to stop showing love to our family. He's calling us to show honor and love in the most meaningful (and sometimes most difficult) ways possible.

Maybe that seems like a hard standard to live up to. These next words of Jesus won't make that seem any easier:

Matthew 5:20—*"I tell you that unless your righteousness surpasses that of the Pharisees and the teachers of the law, you will certainly not enter the kingdom of heaven."*

You've had a hard day. You tried to share words of Christian hope and comfort with a friend who is going through a hard time and she lashed out at you. You came home to your family, needing to spend some time together in God's Word. Instead, you took the easy way out and spent the night in front of the TV together. As you lie down for the night, you decide to finally open your Bible for a little bit of comfort and forgiveness. And what does Jesus tell you? Unless you're more righteous than the most holy-seeming religious leader, you won't enter heaven. Isn't this the same Jesus who said, "God so loved the world that he gave his one and only Son, that whoever *believes* in him shall not perish but have eternal life"? How can he now say something so different?

We'll encounter this truth again and again: Context matters. Just a few verses earlier, Jesus told the people: "Do not think that I have come to abolish the Law or the Prophets; I have not come to abolish them but to fulfill them. I tell you the truth, until heaven and earth disappear, not the smallest letter, not the least stroke of a pen, will by any means disappear from the Law until everything is accomplished" (Matthew 5:17,18). Jesus erases our guilt; he doesn't erase right and wrong. And yes, the only way to belong in heaven is to keep every bit of God's law perfectly, to have a righteousness beyond what even the Pharisees could muster.

Maybe that makes you want to run and hide or bury your head. Good! That's what God wants us to do when he points out our sins. Run to Jesus, and hide in his righteousness. It will cover every one of your sins. Bury your head in the waters of your baptism. There you'll find cleansing for every one of your sins. At the end of your hard day, run to Jesus and he'll tell you: "Through faith in Christ, you have perfect righteousness and the kingdom of heaven is yours!"

Sleep well in that truth. May it give you peace when you lie down and strength for another day of following Jesus, no matter the cost.

3 "Blessed Are Those Who Mourn"

God, it's not fair! I can't believe in a God who lets things like this happen to the people who believe in him!

It probably wouldn't surprise you to hear a discouraged believer speak like that. Maybe it doesn't surprise you when you find yourself thinking like that from time to time. But would it surprise you to read words like that in the Bible? Spoken by one of God's inspired writers?

That's exactly what we find in Psalm 73. Asaph, the inspired writer, loves God. He holds to God's Word and believes it. And he looks at life and sees wicked people getting ahead and getting what they want, while his life is filled with troubles: "As for me, my feet had almost slipped." *God, I was ready to stop believing in you.* It would be hard to imagine a believer thinking that way—except we often do.

That struggle is good. In fact, in the Beatitudes, Jesus *invites* us to struggle with those truths. He says:

Matthew 5:3-12 (NIV 2011)—
"*Blessed are the poor in spirit,*
  for theirs is the kingdom of heaven.
Blessed are those who mourn,
  for they will be comforted.
Blessed are the meek,
  for they will inherit the earth.
Blessed are those who hunger and thirst for righteousness,
  for they will be filled.
Blessed are the merciful,
  for they will be shown mercy.
Blessed are the pure in heart,
  for they will see God.
Blessed are the peacemakers,
  for they will be called children of God.
Blessed are those who are persecuted because of righteousness,
  for theirs is the kingdom of heaven.

Blessed are you when people insult you, persecute you and falsely say all kinds of evil against you because of me. Rejoice and be glad, because great is your reward in heaven, for in the same way they persecuted the prophets who were before you."

Could there be any words that our hearts would struggle with more? The Greek word *blessed* also means "happy." How is there happiness in mourning? being meek? facing persecution for the sake of God's Word?

The world pays lip service to some of the attitudes that Jesus mentions here. The world talks about mercy and peace and purity as good things . . . to a point. But does it really believe this? When mercy and peace invite mockery and abuse, the world is quick to advise a different set of qualities. The true, natural attitude of this world (and of us all by nature) reads more like this:

Blessed are the strong, for they won't be taken advantage of.

Blessed are they who have what their hearts desire, for they will never mourn.

Blessed are the ones who know what they want and will do what it takes to achieve it.

Need we go on?

And living that way seems to make sense! If you doubt that, apply yourself again to living according to the Beatitudes. Doesn't that invite pain from this world? sadness and loss? Doesn't it make you want to cry out, "As for me, my feet had almost slipped"?

That's when you need to finish reading Psalm 73: "When I tried to understand all this, it troubled me deeply till I entered the sanctuary of God; then I understood their final destiny" (verses 16,17 [NIV 2011]).

This world is broken, and it operates according to a broken set of rules. But this isn't the only world. When you remember that, God changes our perspective. That's what Jesus wants us to see in the Beatitudes! The world invites us to find happiness and blessing in self-fulfillment and personal advancement, no matter the cost. But the "rules" of this world are a lie! God is the one who made all things, and he says that real life and real blessings are found in truth, in love, in sacrifice and service. Those things might not always bring us joy and peace now, but when we stand in heaven, we'll see the truth of Jesus' words.

Do you doubt that? Then go to Jesus' Passion Week. The One who embodied meekness and hungering for righteousness was beaten and killed. It looked like the ways of this world had won. But Jesus rose. He rose and lives and rules to bring his people home to an eternity of joy with him. Jesus' promises to us in the Beatitudes are true.

But don't they contradict other parts of Scripture?

Matthew 5:38-42 (NIV 2011)—*"You have heard that it was said, 'Eye for eye, and tooth for tooth.' But I tell you, do not resist an evil person. If anyone slaps you on the right cheek, turn to them the other cheek also. And if anyone wants to sue you and take your shirt, hand over your coat as well. If anyone forces you to go one mile, go with them two miles. Give to the one who asks you, and do not turn away from the one who wants to borrow from you."*

"You have heard that it was said." And we have. The command to take an "eye for eye, and tooth for tooth" is given by God in the Bible. Two times![1] The Bible is clearly telling us to do this, and Jesus is clearly telling us elsewhere in the Bible not to do this. So what's a believer to do with that contradiction?

Study it! Listen to what God is saying! When those words were given in the Old Testament, God gave them as his instructions to *the government of Israel.* They were part of a civil law code by which the government was to function. That law code served the same purpose as one of our guiding principles today: The punishment should fit the crime. With those words, God told the government to protect a victim from not receiving justice and to protect the criminal from receiving an excessive punishment. God wanted the government to be just and fair.

However, human hearts always look for a way to twist God's Word. These commands were spoken to the government, to rein in the government from excessive or unfair punishment. Over the years,

---

[1] Leviticus 24:20 and Deuteronomy 19:21.

people read those words as if God were giving them permission to seek out personal vengeance. Words meant to protect the guilty became an excuse to harm them.

God does want the government to keep law and order and to bring about justice. That's *the government's* role. But as believing children of God, we have a different concern. Our first concern isn't bringing about justice for the wrongdoer. It isn't about getting even. It's showing love and mercy.

Struggle with those words! When someone harms you, you need to live as an inhabitant of earth and a citizen of heaven. As an inhabitant of earth, you know that God wants to preserve order. So let the law courts bring about a just punishment when the situation calls for it. That's the government's business. And remember yours. Your business is the same as that of the one who looked down from a cross and prayed, "Father, forgive them, for they do not know what they are doing." Your business is mercy and forgiveness.

And sometimes that business will take more strength than you could ever imagine!

> **Matthew 5:43-48 (NIV 2011)**—*"You have heard that it was said, 'Love your neighbor and hate your enemy.' But I tell you, love your enemies and pray for those who persecute you, that you may be children of your Father in heaven. He causes his sun to rise on the evil and the good, and sends rain on the righteous and the unrighteous. If you love those who love you, what reward will you get? Are not even the tax collectors doing that? And if you greet only your own people, what are you doing more than others? Do not even pagans do that? Be perfect, therefore, as your heavenly Father is perfect."*

Those last words lay a heavy burden on us. Jesus sets a high standard. He doesn't just say, *"Love."* He says, *"Love. Your enemies. Perfectly."*

The Beatitudes that we've looked at in this section are some of the most quoted and most loved sayings of Jesus. They are beautiful! But they are crushing and damning words too. If we show love to our families and our friends, our neighbors and those in our community, Jesus still looks at us and says, "Fine! You are acting like a wonderful pagan!" Acting like a child of God means *loving* the people who are hurting you most, praying for those who are cursing you, and doing all of this perfectly. Struggle with those words of Jesus, because they show us that the real struggle is with our own sinful hearts. Who can live this way?

If you feel crushed by the Beatitudes at all, then let them build you back up. Look again at Jesus' words: "But I tell you, love your enemies and pray for those who persecute you, that you may be children of *your Father* in heaven." You don't face this alone. You have a Father in heaven who has shown this love to you already. You have a Father in heaven who is there to give you strength and forgiveness.

Asaph, the man who penned Psalm 73, struggled with what it meant to live as a child of God in an unfair, unbelieving world. The struggle was good. It got him to think about what really matters, how this world really works, and where his treasure really was. Struggle together with him. Let Jesus' words in the Beatitudes push you to consider how far *love* and *mercy* really go. And then as you find comfort in your Father's love, say with Asaph, "Whom have I in heaven but you? And earth has nothing I desire besides you" (Psalm 73:25).

"Out of Men's Hearts Comes Evil"

Are you a good person or a bad person? It's a very simple question that's very difficult for most people to answer. Are we born into this world as blank slates, molded and shaped by our experiences into someone *good* or someone *bad?* Are some inclined towards evil and others inclined towards virtue?

Different cultures and societies answer that question in different ways. In the United States, one answer seems to have won the day: *People are basically good.*

It's a comfortable answer. I like the thought that, even though I'm not perfect, "I'm basically a good guy." I like the thought that the people I love and the people with whom I share desk space at work are basically good.

It's a comfortable answer, but it doesn't satisfy. If we're all basically good, then why is there so much hatred and wrong in the world? If I'm basically good, why do I keep doing things that are wrong? If I'm basically good, then why do I feel so guilty sometimes?

Mark 7:14-23—*Again Jesus called the crowd to him and said, "Listen to me, everyone, and understand this. Nothing outside a man can make him 'unclean' by going into him. Rather, it is what comes out of a man that makes him 'unclean.'" After he had left the crowd and entered the house, his disciples asked him about this parable. "Are you so dull?" he asked. "Don't you see that nothing that enters a man from the outside can make him 'unclean'? For it doesn't go into his heart but into his stomach, and then out of his body." (In saying this, Jesus declared all foods "clean.") He went on: "What comes out of a man is what makes him 'unclean.' For from within, out of men's hearts, come evil thoughts, sexual immorality, theft, murder, adultery, greed, malice, deceit, lewdness, envy, slander, arrogance and folly. All these evils come from inside and make a man 'unclean.'"*

It started off as a question about an Old Testament ceremonial law. God instructed the Israelites to take part in certain ceremonial washings. Those washings were pictures—daily reminders of the need for cleansing from sin. Over the centuries, the religious elders of Israel had expanded those laws to mandate ceremonial washings before consuming any food. What was intended as a picture of sin and forgiveness became a checklist for being a good person.

Jesus' argument is simple, basic, and undeniable. Food (even food eaten with unwashed hands) can't make you "clean" or "unclean," "good" or "evil." You eat it, and a few hours later it passes out of your body.

It's a simple enough point, but Jesus used it as a chance to teach a much harder truth. If evil doesn't come from what we bring inside us, then where does it come from? "Out of men's hearts . . . come evil thoughts, sexual immorality, theft, murder, adultery, greed, malice, deceit, lewdness, envy, slander, arrogance and folly" (Mark 7:21,22). Evil comes from within us. We aren't basically good. All of the evil in the world comes from human hearts. It comes from my heart and yours.

It's no wonder our world struggles with that teaching and rejects it! To admit that I'm by nature an "object of wrath"[2] and "hostile to God"[3] is to give up every bit of pride and every self-image I have of being a "basically good person." It's to cry, "Lord, have mercy on me, a sinner!"

That doesn't mean that other peoples' sins don't affect us. They certainly do! Jesus warns against leading others into sin.[4] If we grow up in homes where certain sins are common or accepted, it does shape and influence us. But even at those times, our sins are just that: they're *our* sins, springing from *our* hearts.

Struggle with those words. Jesus is challenging us to see ourselves in a way we should want to run from. We are the source of evil in this world. But can you deny it? Even a "Christian nation" like the United States is filled with victims of sexual abuse, broken marriages, and lives destroyed by greed. We witnessed the horror of Jesus' words in the last century, as so many "good, churchgoing people" committed

---

[2] Ephesians 2:3.
[3] Romans 8:7.
[4] Matthew 18:6.

unspeakable atrocities in the concentration camps of Nazi Germany. Evil lurks within us all.

But maybe that kind of evil seems far off. So Jesus uses an inescapable part of our daily lives to explain a truth we'd rather avoid.

> **Matthew 6:19-24**—*"Do not store up for yourselves treasures on earth, where moth and rust destroy, and where thieves break in and steal. But store up for yourselves treasures in heaven, where moth and rust do not destroy, and where thieves do not break in and steal. For where your treasure is, there your heart will be also. The eye is the lamp of the body. If your eyes are good, your whole body will be full of light. But if your eyes are bad, your whole body will be full of darkness. If then the light within you is darkness, how great is that darkness! No one can serve two masters. Either he will hate the one and love the other, or he will be devoted to the one and despise the other. You cannot serve both God and Money."*

So much of our lives is organized around the pursuit of money. We can't function in our culture without it. It's a necessary tool. And it doesn't seem like pursuing money would keep us from loving God. Would Jesus have us believe that applying for a better job threatens our faith? that taking a promotion at work means demoting our faith?

Take a close look at the kinds of words Jesus uses here. He talks about *love* for money. He talks about *serving* material wealth. Those are heart words. They have nothing to do with how little money or how much money you have. Jesus is talking about how we feel about money. Jesus would have us ask: *What is the organizing principle of my life? What does my life revolve around? What guides my decisions?* And very often, money subtly becomes the answer.

But keep reading Jesus' words:

> "Therefore I tell you, do not worry about your life, what you will eat or drink; or about your body, what you will wear. Is not life more important than food, and the body more important than clothes? Look at the birds of the air; they do not sow or reap or store away in barns, and yet your heavenly Father feeds them. Are you not much more valuable than they?" (Matthew 6:25,26)

Jesus gives us this warning because he wants to give us a great blessing: He wants us to be free from worry. How do you get that blessing? You won't find it in any amount of money. But keep God in first place in your life. Make his Word more important than extra shifts at work or the stack of bills that weighs on you. In his Word, God will show you just how much he loves you—enough to give his own Son for you. Enough to *make you his child.* Can you imagine that? It leads us to rejoice in the truth: "He who did not spare his own Son, but gave him up for us all—how will he not also, along with him, graciously give us all things?"[5]

Food. Clothes. Money. Our careers. Our wants and our needs. Jesus speaks about all of these things. And what he has to say is hard to hear. He calls us to face the fact that our hearts are by nature poison wells that flood this world with sin. He warns us and pleads with us about how easily our hearts put the stuff of this life before our eternal God. But read over these verses again and you'll see the amazing truth behind his warning. These sinful hearts? These hearts that love money? Jesus wants those hearts more than anything. He wants our hearts to be healed and at peace with him. He isn't just trying to control our actions. He's come to make our hearts clean and give us peace. We may have been born into this world as "bad people," but we have a good God who is there to graciously forgive and renew us. It's as a church father, St. Augustine, once prayed, *"You made us for yourself, Lord, and our hearts are restless until they rest in you."*[6]

---

[5]Romans 8:32.
[6]From *The Confessions of St. Augustine,* book 1, paragraph 1.

"I Am Coming Back Soon"

Hebrews 13:5—*"Never will I leave you; never will I forsake you."*

Isaiah 1:18—*"Though your sins are like scarlet, they shall be as white as snow."*

Matthew 6:33—*"Seek first his kingdom and his righteousness, and all these things will be given to you as well."*

God's promises are a warm blanket in which we wrap our souls. They give us such great comfort because we know they're true. We read his Word, and we know God is with us. We listen to the accounts of those who saw Jesus after he rose from the dead, and we know our sins are indeed forgiven. Even when life is hard and resources are stretched, every day is proof that God will always keep his promise to give us what we need for this life.

But what if Jesus spoke a promise that was simple and clear . . . and didn't keep it?

Mark 8:34–9:1—*Then he called the crowd to him along with his disciples and said: "If anyone would come after me, he must deny himself and take up his cross and follow me. For whoever wants to save his life will lose it, but whoever loses his life for me and for the gospel will save it. What good is it for a man to gain the whole world, yet forfeit his soul? Or what can a man give in exchange for his soul? If anyone is ashamed of me and my words in this adulterous and sinful generation, the Son of Man will be ashamed of him when he comes in his Father's glory with the holy angels." And he said to them, "I tell you the truth, some who are standing here will not taste death before they see the kingdom of God come with power."*

Some of Jesus' promises about his return to judge the world and take believers home give us reason to struggle to understand him. He talks about returning "soon."[7] It's been more than two thousand years! But believers hold to the way God explains his own words: "The Lord is not slow in keeping his promise, as some understand slowness. He is patient with you, not wanting anyone to perish, but everyone to come to repentance."[8] In God's time frame, two thousand years ago his return would be "soon." And it's still coming "soon" now.

But this promise is different. After predicting his own death, Jesus reminds his disciples that he is still the Savior whom God promised and that he will not fail. In his encouragement, Jesus seems to be saying that *some disciples who were alive two thousand years ago will still be alive when he comes back.* And this promise isn't just recorded for us once; Matthew and Luke record it for us as well.

You can understand why critics of the Bible take issue with this promise. As far as we know, there aren't any two-thousand-year-old people walking around, waiting for Jesus' return. The critics' explanation is simple and logical. They believe that Jesus *always* taught his disciples to believe that he would return within a few years (or decades, at most) after his ascension. When that didn't take place, the church *had* to change its teaching. It began to reinterpret Jesus' promises simply to mean we should always be ready for an imminent return.

Consider what's at stake. If the critics are correct, then believers have put their faith in a fabrication, a lie. If Jesus did teach that he would return during the disciples' lifetimes, then he was a liar. We'd have every reason to look at Jesus' promises and consider them broken.

But before you consider them broken, consider them carefully and thoughtfully. There's a reason the church has marked a chapter break between Mark 8:38 and 9:1. At the end of chapter 8, Jesus is clearly talking about his second coming. Some people then naturally assume he's still talking about his return for judgment in 9:1. He's not. As you think about Jesus' promise about "the kingdom of God com[ing] with power," consider these other statements of Jesus:

---

[7] Revelation 22:20.
[8] 2 Peter 3:9.

> **Luke 17:20,21 (ESV)**—*Being asked by the Pharisees when the kingdom of God would come, he answered them, "The kingdom of God is not coming in ways that can be observed, nor will they say, 'Look, here it is!' or 'There!' for behold, the kingdom of God is in the midst of you."*[9]
>
> **Luke 24:46-49**—*[Jesus] told them, "This is what is written: The Christ will suffer and rise from the dead on the third day, and repentance and forgiveness of sins will be preached in his name to all nations, beginning at Jerusalem. You are witnesses of these things. I am going to send you what my Father has promised; but stay in the city until you have been clothed with power from on high."*
>
> **I Thessalonians 1:4,5**—*We know, brothers loved by God, that he has chosen you, because our gospel came to you not simply with words, but also with power, with the Holy Spirit and with deep conviction. You know how we lived among you for your sake.*

When we think of a kingdom, humans think about armies and fortresses and visible conquests. Jesus doesn't. And he tells us not to. The kingdom of God *isn't* just what we'll see when Jesus comes again in glory. It's what happens whenever God's forgiveness and mercy is preached. When it comes, it isn't visible to the human eye (Luke 17:20) but is still all around us (Luke 17:21). It's found in the preaching of Jesus' forgiveness, starting on the day of Pentecost as Christ poured out his Spirit (Luke 24:49). And whenever that message is preached, it still is filled with God's power (I Thessalonians 1:5).

That's what Jesus promised his disciples. Yes, they would see Jesus killed. Yes, following Jesus would come at a cost. Yes, all of this would finally come to an end on the Last Day. But they didn't have to wait until then to have peace. During their own lives, they'd see the real power of God's kingdom.

And you see it too. We want Jesus to come back. We want an end to the pain and injustice that so often fill this world. But, Jesus says, see more than that! In the preaching of the gospel, in sinners repent-

---

[9] The English Standard Version is quoted here because "in the midst of you" is a preferable translation to the NIV 1984's "within you."

ing of their ways, in troubled consciences finding forgiveness and peace—each and every day the promises of Christ are shared!—Jesus is reigning with power.

But that doesn't mean we should stop thinking about the end!

The Signs of the End

While Jesus' reign in our hearts is invisible, he gives us visible signs to remind us of his promise to return and redeem this world.

Mark 13:5-31—*Jesus said to them: "Watch out that no one deceives you. Many will come in my name, claiming, 'I am he,' and will deceive many. When you hear of wars and rumors of wars, do not be alarmed. Such things must happen, but the end is still to come. Nation will rise against nation, and kingdom against kingdom. There will be earthquakes in various places, and famines. These are the beginning of birth pains. You must be on your guard. You will be handed over to the local councils and flogged in the synagogues. On account of me you will stand before governors and kings as witnesses to them. And the gospel must first be preached to all nations. Whenever you are arrested and brought to trial, do not worry beforehand about what to say. Just say whatever is given you at the time, for it is not you speaking, but the Holy Spirit. Brother will betray brother to death, and a father his child. Children will rebel against their parents and have them put to death. All men will hate you because of me, but he who stands firm to the end will be saved. When you see 'the abomination that causes desolation' standing where it does not belong—let the reader understand—then let those who are in Judea flee to the mountains. Let no one on the roof of his house go down or enter the house to take anything out. Let no one in the field go back to get his cloak. How dreadful it will be in those days for pregnant women and nursing mothers! Pray that this will not take place in winter, because those will be days of distress unequaled from the beginning, when God created the world, until now—and never to be equaled again. If the Lord had not cut short those days, no one would survive. But for the sake of the elect, whom he has chosen, he has shortened them. At that time if anyone says to you, 'Look, here is the Christ!' or, 'Look, there he is!' do not believe it. For false Christs and false* *prophets will appear and perform signs and miracles to deceive the elect—if that were possible. So be on your guard; I have told you everything ahead of time. But in those days, following that distress, 'the sun will be darkened, and the moon will not give its light; the stars will fall from the sky, and the heavenly bodies will be shaken.' At that time men will see the Son of Man coming in clouds with great power and glory. And he will send his angels and gather his elect from the four winds, from the ends of the earth to the ends of the heavens. Now learn this lesson from the fig tree: As soon as its twigs get tender and its leaves come out, you know that summer is near. Even so, when you see these things happening, you know that it is near, right at the door. I tell you the truth, this generation will certainly not pass away until all these things have happened. Heaven and earth will pass away, but my words will never pass away."*

Earthquakes! Wars! False Christs! When you see these things, be prepared for the end of the world! And that *is* what Christ was saying. These signs were finding fulfillment even in "this generation" that the disciples were living in (Mark 13:30).

Any time you see these signs being fulfilled, be ready. But *don't* expect to use them as a countdown to Christ's return. We're again living in a time where much of popular Christianity seeks to use these signs and other sections of Scripture to predict when the end of the world will be. The point of these signs isn't to tell us when the end is coming; they're reminders to always be ready.

If you doubt that, just keep reading. Let Jesus himself explain. He goes on to say:

Mark 13:32-37—*"No one knows about that day or hour, not even the angels in heaven, nor the Son, but only the Father. Be on guard! Be alert! You do not know when that time will come. It's like a man going away: He leaves his house and puts his servants in charge, each with his assigned task, and tells the one at the door to keep watch. Therefore keep watch because you do not know when the owner of the house will come back—whether in the evening, or at midnight, or when the rooster crows, or at dawn. If he comes suddenly, do not let him find you sleeping. What I say to you, I say to everyone: 'Watch!'"*

The angels don't know the day or hour. In his state of humility, Jesus himself didn't know the day or hour. Neither will you. That information is entrusted to the Father alone. So don't worry about what you don't know. Rejoice in what you do know. You know the Savior who has redeemed you from your sin and has prepared a home in heaven for you. You know Jesus. And you know he hasn't forgotten you.

Does it feel like it? When you have aches and pains, when you see yet another war break out, when you bury a parent or a child, when you just want to be home in heaven, do you wonder why God hasn't come back yet?

It's because he loves you.

Jesus' "Delay" Shows His Love

John 21:20-23—*Peter turned and saw that the disciple whom Jesus loved was following them. (This was the one who had leaned back against Jesus at the supper and had said, "Lord, who is going to betray you?") When Peter saw him, he asked, "Lord, what about him?" Jesus answered, "If I want him to remain alive until I return, what is that to you? You must follow me." Because of this, the rumor spread among the brothers that this disciple would not die. But Jesus did not say that he would not die; he only said, "If I want him to remain alive until I return, what is that to you?"*

Maybe it seems like a small thing—even something to chuckle about. Some of the disciples thought Jesus meant that John wouldn't die until Jesus' return. But what did they think on the day John *did* die? Did they wonder what that meant about Jesus' promise?

Little misunderstandings like that can cause great struggles! Consider the one facing Christians in Thessalonica:

> Brothers, we do not want you to be ignorant about those who fall asleep, or to grieve like the rest of men, who have no hope. We believe that Jesus died and rose again and so we believe that God will bring with Jesus those who have

fallen asleep in him. According to the Lord's own word, we tell you that we who are still alive, who are left till the coming of the Lord, will certainly not precede those who have fallen asleep. (1 Thessalonians 4:13-15)

Somehow the Thessalonian Christians had come to believe that if a believer died before Jesus came back, he or she would miss out on the resurrection. What horrible sadness and hopelessness they faced as they buried their mothers, their husbands, and their friends! They must have been confused—even angry!—that Jesus hadn't come back sooner.

There's a good reason he hasn't. "The Lord is not slow in keeping his promise, as some understand slowness. He is patient with you, not wanting anyone to perish, but everyone to come to repentance" (2 Peter 3:9). Jesus said "soon," but two thousand years later he still hasn't come back. If you ever wonder if the critics are correct in thinking that this is one promise Jesus simply didn't keep, run back to these words. Jesus hasn't failed to keep his promise. He isn't slow in keeping his promise. Why hasn't he come back yet?

Because of you. Because you're worth waiting for. Because if he would have returned 1,900 years ago, you wouldn't have been born and wouldn't have come to know God's promises. He waited this long to save you. Will he wait longer? It's not out of slowness. It's because he's waiting for a few more. And then, when the last one is brought to faith, he'll come back. You know when that day will be.

It'll be *soon*.

"IF YOU HAVE FAITH AS SMALL AS A MUSTARD SEED . . . NOTHING WILL BE IMPOSSIBLE FOR YOU"

This is the age of the *nones*.

If you haven't heard the term before, the *nones* are people who claim no religious affiliation. They don't belong to a church or denomination. And their numbers are on the rise.

Some have heralded this as the end of religion in the United States,[10] but other facts stubbornly argue against that. Within the group of people who claim no church affiliation, people still overwhelmingly identify themselves as "spiritual" or "religious." They want faith, but they don't want what they see in the church.

Maybe you can sympathize with them. How many scandals have rocked the flock? How many shepherds have been revealed to be wolves in sheep's clothing? How many times have people learned the teachings of their church, only to have their church change its doctrine? "What we used to tell you was God's truth? We've changed our minds. You don't need to believe that anymore. Now *this* is what God says."

But perhaps that's only half of it. As our world has grown more connected, we get a better view of what's going on around us every day. It isn't pretty! God promises to watch over his little flock, but Christians are so often persecuted. He tells us that all things will work for our good, but so much seems to be spinning out of control. It's a natural human reaction to view faith like a poker game: Only gamble what you're willing to lose. Don't put too much faith in God's promises and it won't hurt so much if they don't seem to come true. Don't risk taking a stand on God's Word; just be "spiritual."

Is faith a poker game and a gamble? If it feels that way, just watch as Jesus ups the ante.

---

[10]http://www.huffingtonpost.com/gary-laderman/the-rise-of-religious-non_b_2913000.html

Jesus Makes Unbelievable Promises About Faith

Matthew 17:14-20—*When they came to the crowd, a man approached Jesus and knelt before him. "Lord, have mercy on my son," he said. "He has seizures and is suffering greatly. He often falls into the fire or into the water. I brought him to your disciples, but they could not heal him." "O unbelieving and perverse generation," Jesus replied, "how long shall I stay with you? How long shall I put up with you? Bring the boy here to me." Jesus rebuked the demon, and it came out of the boy, and he was healed from that moment. Then the disciples came to Jesus in private and asked, "Why couldn't we drive it out?" He replied, "Because you have so little faith. I tell you the truth, if you have faith as small as a mustard seed, you can say to this mountain, 'Move from here to there' and it will move. Nothing will be impossible for you."*

The disciples went about the work Jesus gave them. He told them to drive out demons,[11] so they went to do so. But this time it didn't work. If they were confused by their failure, they must have been baffled by Jesus' response. They had "so little faith." And to underscore his point, Jesus talked of mustard seeds and mountains and the true power that faith has.

It sounds beautiful, but it feels false. After all, haven't you prayed, truly believing God would grant it, and not seen it happen? Haven't you had faith that everything would work out in one way, only to see it all fall apart?

Sometimes this gracious promise of Jesus seems absolutely devastating! Perhaps you've thought this way before: *Jesus said that if we just have faith as small as a mustard seed, nothing will be impossible. And I do believe! But I wasn't able to do what I wanted. I didn't conquer that temptation. I didn't witness as clearly as I wanted. My prayers weren't answered. I guess my faith is too small. I failed.*

Faith is just that: it's faith. It isn't a magic wand that we wave over our wish lists to bring them into reality. It isn't a spell that we

---

[11]Matthew 10:1.

use to bend God's will to our own. *Faith is simple trust in God's promises to us.*

Jesus sent the disciples to drive out demons. This is what he told them: "Heal the sick, raise the dead, cleanse those who have leprosy, drive out demons."[12] He told them he was giving them the power to do these things. He gave them his promise. And, to their shame, the disciples seemed to fail to trust that promise as they went about their work.

Faith is trust in God's promises. That means we need to know what his promises are! If God gave you the command to move mountains and promised you the power to do so, trust in those promises and it will happen! But he hasn't given you that command or promise. Has Jesus given you the promise that you can heal those who have leprosy? No! It's not "faith" to think that you can do it—and it's not a failure of faith if you *can't* do it. You don't have that promise from God. Do you want to conquer a temptation? succeed at a new endeavor in life? recover from your cancer? Remember God's promises to you. He hasn't promised that you'll always succeed in any one of those things. Maybe you will fail! But that's not the same as your faith failing, because God's promises to you still stand. If you fall into sin again, he promises to forgive you. If your best efforts fall apart, he promises he'll still provide. If you lose the battle to cancer and fall asleep in Christ, he promises to take you home to heaven. Faith holds to God's promises, not our own plans.

But what about the blank checks Jesus gives us? Read through John chapters 14 and 15, and you'll find them repeated:

John 14:14—*"You may ask me for anything in my name, and I will do it."*

John 15:7—*"If you remain in me and my words remain in you, ask whatever you wish, and it will be given you."*

John 15:16—*"Then the Father will give you whatever you ask in my name."*

---

[12] Matthew 10:8.

What incredible promises! Take them to heart! Go to Jesus with your earnest prayers and trust in his gracious love.

But . . . what about the times the Father doesn't give us what we ask for? when Jesus doesn't do what we ask? Every believer knows the experience of praying for something that seems to be good and right, truly wanting it and truly believing God will give it, and coming up empty-handed. It feels like Jesus' blank checks bounced. And we seem to be left with only two reactions: *(1) Maybe I'm not really "remaining in Jesus." I must not be a good enough Christian; it's my fault.* Or *(2) Jesus isn't really keeping his promises. He must not have meant this. It must be his fault.*

At a time like that, ask yourself: *What am I really praying for?* At its heart, every believer's prayer is the same, whether we're praying for a child to come back to faith, a parent to get better, a promotion to come at work, or a disease to leave our bodies. The prayer is always: *God, bless me. Do what's best for me.*

Jesus will always answer that prayer. He will always bless us. If he knows that a few more years on earth for our parents would bring them pain instead of joy, he might answer our prayers by bringing them home. If he knows that the promotion at work would be a curse to our families instead of a blessing, he might bless us by guarding our homes by keeping us from that promotion. But he'll do what's best. And, at its heart, isn't that what our prayers seek?

Jesus' Faithful Prayer Bolsters Our Faith in His Promises

Matthew 26:36-46—*Then Jesus went with his disciples to a place called Gethsemane, and he said to them, "Sit here while I go over there and pray." He took Peter and the two sons of Zebedee along with him, and he began to be sorrowful and troubled. Then he said to them, "My soul is overwhelmed with sorrow to the point of death. Stay here and keep watch with me." Going a little farther, he fell with his face to the ground and prayed, "My Father, if it is possible, may this cup be taken from me. Yet not as I will, but as you will." Then he returned to his disciples and found them sleeping. "Could you men not keep watch*

> with me for one hour?" he asked Peter. "Watch and pray so that you will not fall into temptation. The spirit is willing, but the body is weak." He went away a second time and prayed, "My Father, if it is not possible for this cup to be taken away unless I drink it, may your will be done." When he came back, he again found them sleeping, because their eyes were heavy. So he left them and went away once more and prayed the third time, saying the same thing. Then he returned to the disciples and said to them, "Are you still sleeping and resting? Look, the hour is near, and the Son of Man is betrayed into the hands of sinners. Rise, let us go! Here comes my betrayer!"

If you struggle in your prayer life, you aren't alone. Jesus did too. With all his heart, he wanted to avoid the suffering and pain that was waiting for him on the cross. He was overwhelmed with sorrow to the point of death. St. Luke even describes Jesus' prayerful sweat, falling to the ground like great drops of blood.[13] He was committed to saving the world but was crushed under the cost that came with it.

His cross was different than ours, but his prayer is the same one you've prayed countless times. *God, work out your loving will. And bless me as you do. Remember your faithful love to me.* Less than 24 hours later, Jesus was dead. The Son who spoke to his Father in prayer cried out, *"Why have you forsaken me?"* The cup didn't pass from him; he drank every last poison drop.

Did the Father answer Jesus' prayer? The answer was as undeniable as the sunrise on Easter Sunday morning. The Father didn't grant Jesus' petition to have the cup of suffering pass from him, because it couldn't. There was no other way to pay for the world's sins but through the suffering and death of God himself. But the Father remembered his faithful love. Jesus committed his spirit into his Father's hands, and God remembered his faithful love to his Son. He granted him the salvation of the world. And on the third day, Jesus rose in triumph. God's will was done. He had blessed his Son and had won blessings for all his sons and daughters.

---

[13] Luke 22:44.

Faith isn't a gamble. Prayer isn't a poker game. It's trust in God's promises. Sometimes those promises seem absolutely unbelievable. And sometimes, what we see in the church, in the world, or in our own lives will confuse us or cause us to struggle. When we feel that way, there's no better place to be than in the garden with Jesus. He struggled in prayer—not because God isn't faithful but because sometimes life is hard and what we *want* isn't what will *bless* us. So struggle with those promises too. Hold to them. Then follow Jesus from the garden to the cross and remember what God wants most of all: our salvation. And stand with Jesus on Easter Sunday morning and rejoice to say, "Father, you have blessed me and you love me."

7   "No One Is Good—Except God Alone"

It was like two boards glued together.
It was like the way a soul fills a body.
It was like when a character on a stage wears a mask.

How do you describe what happened when God became man? All three of those statements are versions of false teachings that came up in the early church. Some taught that Jesus was half God, half man (like two boards glued together). Others thought the "divine essence" simply inhabited a human body (as our souls do) without truly becoming human. Or perhaps Jesus was God simply "pretending" to be man, so we could have courage to approach him (much like the actor on a stage plays a part).

The question isn't just idle speculation or a theological exercise. We see how important this question is when we're faced with the question, Who died on the cross? Who was this Jesus?

At Times, Jesus Seemed to Say He Was Less Than God

It was early on the first Easter morning. Jesus had just achieved his greatest triumph—but his people didn't know it yet. Some disciples had seen the empty tomb and had left with questions. Now Mary had the privilege of being the first to see her risen Lord and Savior. She came face-to-face with the truth that Jesus is God himself, with power over death.

> **John 20:11-17**—*Mary stood outside the tomb crying. As she wept, she bent over to look into the tomb and saw two angels in white, seated where Jesus' body had been, one at the head and the other at the foot. They asked her, "Woman, why are you crying?" "They have taken my Lord away," she said, "and I don't know where they have put him." At this, she turned around and saw Jesus standing there, but she did not realize that it was Jesus. "Woman," he said,*

"No One Is Good—Except God Alone"

"why are you crying? Who is it you are looking for?" Thinking he was the gardener, she said, "Sir, if you have carried him away, tell me where you have put him, and I will get him." Jesus said to her, "Mary." She turned toward him and cried out in Aramaic, "Rabboni!" (which means Teacher). Jesus said, "Do not hold on to me, for I have not yet returned to the Father. Go instead to my brothers and tell them, 'I am returning to my Father and your Father, to my God and your God.'"

What a perfect time for Jesus to trumpet his divinity. *Mary, your God stands in front of you in victory!* So why, then, does Jesus refer to the Father as "my God"?

This isn't the only time Jesus talked that way. Consider the following passages:

Mark 10:17,18—*As Jesus started on his way, a man ran up to him and fell on his knees before him. "Good teacher," he asked, "what must I do to inherit eternal life?" "Why do you call me good?" Jesus answered. "No one is good—except God alone."*

John 14:28,31—*"You heard me say, 'I am going away and I am coming back to you.' If you loved me, you would be glad that I am going to the Father, for the Father is greater than I. . . . The world must learn that I love the Father and that I do exactly what my Father has commanded me."*

John 8:28,29—*So Jesus said, "When you have lifted up the Son of Man, then you will know that I am the one I claim to be and that I do nothing on my own but speak just what the Father has taught me. The one who sent me is with me; he has not left me alone, for I always do what pleases him."*

Don't call Jesus good because only God is good? Jesus is God himself, equal to the Father, yet the Father is greater than he is? Jesus can't do anything on his own but only what the Father has taught him? That's not the way you'd expect God to speak!

We can find help in God's Word to the Christians in Philippi:

Philippians 2:5-8—*Your attitude should be the same as that of Christ Jesus: Who, being in very nature God, did not consider equality* with God something to be grasped, but made himself nothing, taking the very nature of a servant, being made in human likeness. And being found in appearance as a man, he humbled himself and became obedient to death—even death on a cross!

Jesus isn't half God. He didn't pretend to be God. The person of Jesus was fully human yet, at the same time, was "in very nature God." Even though he didn't always *seem* to be God—he was "found in appearance as a man"—that's exactly who he is.

We call this portion of Jesus' life his humiliation. He still had full possession of his power and glory as God; he showed that through his miracles and his transfiguration. Yet he didn't make full use of that power. That was Jesus' choice, willingly made out of love for us.

That truth drips in comfort for us. God himself knows what your life is like; his life on earth wasn't playacting. It wasn't just Jesus' "human half" that suffered. Fully God and fully man, he took full part in this life of ours.

And that's what some of his words clearly tell us.

At Times, Jesus Clearly Witnessed to His Divinity

Maybe you've heard it said: "Jesus never claimed to be God." That's technically true; Jesus never said, "I am God." But the statement is also incredibly false.

Mark 2:1-11—*A few days later, when Jesus again entered Capernaum, the people heard that he had come home. So many gathered that there was no room left, not even outside the door, and he preached the word to them. Some men came, bringing to him a paralytic, carried by four of them. Since they could not get him to Jesus because of the crowd, they made an opening in the roof above Jesus and, after digging through it, lowered the mat the paralyzed man was lying on. When Jesus saw their faith, he said to the paralytic, "Son, your sins are forgiven." Now some teachers of the law were sitting there, thinking to themselves, "Why does this fellow talk like that? He's blaspheming! Who can forgive sins* *but God alone?" Immediately Jesus knew in his spirit that this was what they were thinking in their hearts, and he said to them, "Why are you thinking these things? Which is easier: to say to the paralytic, 'Your sins are forgiven,' or to say, 'Get up, take your mat and walk'? But that you may know that the Son of Man has authority on earth to forgive sins. . . ."* He said to the paralytic, *"I tell you, get up, take your mat and go home."*

Don't overthink Jesus' question. Only God can forgive sins. Only God can miraculously cure a paralytic. But it's easier to say, "Your sins are forgiven." *Anyone* can say that; *no one* can tell by observation if it's true or not. But if someone tells a paralyzed man to pick up his mat and walk home, everyone will be able to tell if that someone has the power to grant miracles.

Jesus trapped the teachers of the law in their own thoughts. They rightly understood that the true power to forgive sin lay with God alone. They also knew that no mere man could heal paralyzed limbs with a word. When he showed that he had the power to do what they could see with their eyes, it was proof that he also had the power to forgive sins. By their own thinking, this was proof that Jesus is God himself.

It wasn't the only time that Jesus told them. Consider these statements Jesus made:

John 8:58—*"I tell you the truth," Jesus answered, "before Abraham was born, I am!"*

Jesus told his fellow Jews that he existed before Abraham—a man who had lived nearly two thousand years earlier. But there's more than that in these words. When Jesus said, "I am," he used words that would have been unmistakable to his Jewish audience. God had revealed himself to Moses and the Israelites as "I AM."[14] Jesus' statement was a clear claim to being the God who revealed himself to Moses in the burning bush and who watched over the Israelites during the exodus. And the Jewish people understood what he was saying. When they heard it, they tried to stone him—the

---

[14]Exodus 3:14.

punishment due to anyone committing blasphemy by claiming to be God.

> **John 10:17,18**—*"The reason my Father loves me is that I lay down my life—only to take it up again. No one takes it from me, but I lay it down of my own accord. I have authority to lay it down and authority to take it up again. This command I received from my Father."*

When Jesus laid down his life, he was acting in line with his Father's will. But the "authority" of life and death—even his own life and death—belonged to Jesus. That's the kind of power that only God has.

> **Matthew 26:63,64**—*Jesus remained silent. The high priest said to him, "I charge you under oath by the living God: Tell us if you are the Christ, the Son of God." "Yes, it is as you say," Jesus replied. "But I say to all of you: In the future you will see the Son of Man sitting at the right hand of the Mighty One and coming on the clouds of heaven."*

Jesus clearly calls himself "the Son of God." But that's not the only (or most powerful) claim to divinity in his words here. Jesus often referred to himself as "the Son of Man." Those words don't emphasize his humanity though. In Daniel chapter 7, we see a vision of the Last Day. The God who comes back to judge this world is "one like a son of man" who is given all authority and power. By using those words, Jesus was saying, "I am the God of heaven and earth whom Daniel saw." The people who heard him understood it. And they killed him for it.

Sometimes Jesus sounded as though he were just a man, certainly less than God. He could speak that way because in his humiliation he lowered himself and set aside the use of his power and his glory to save us. According to his humanity, he *was* less than God. But as his words and miracles show, he was still fully God and equal to the Father according to his divinity. He wasn't two boards glued together. He was more than God-in-a-human-body. This was no act.

But back to the question that really matters: Who died on the cross? Jesus did. Jesus, who was truly man. Jesus, who was fully God.

That means God died on the cross.[15] That's the way it had to be. The life of one human (even a perfect human) could not provide fitting payment for the sins of billions of souls. God's life is the only sacrifice that could atone for all those sins. That's what Jesus offered on the cross.

Jesus paid the price that can cover all of your sins—in fact, all of the *world's* sins. What comfort! But it goes further than that. Jesus is still fully God and fully man. That means humanity itself is exalted. The one who sits on heaven's throne is your brother. When we understand who Jesus is, we understand who we are too.

We are part of God's family.

---

[15] The Athanasian Creed is a historic confession of the Christian faith that helps explain this more fully. Consider reading it. Much of this is hard to understand because of the miracle and mystery of our triune God. Jesus is fully God, and he died on the cross for us. That does not mean, however, that the Father or the Spirit died.

8 "UNLESS YOUR RIGHTEOUSNESS SURPASSES THAT OF THE TEACHERS OF THE LAW..."

"One of my friends is a Christian. He goes to church every weekend. He sings in the choir. He even helped out with the youth group's camping trip. But you should hear him talk. Get a few beers in him and he'll cuss a streak. He says the worst things about his wife—and you should hear the things he says about other women! So you're telling me he's going to heaven?"

"You should really meet her—she's an incredible woman. When she's not volunteering at the hospital or library, she's helping out her dad. He's very sick. I don't know how my friend keeps it all going. But you never hear a complaint out of her. She still manages to put a smile on everyone's face. But let me get this straight . . . you believe that because she's not a Christian, she's not going to heaven?"

Most Christians have faced questions like these. And most Christians can probably give a good answer about how salvation comes through faith in Jesus, apart from our works.

But then Jesus speaks. He praises good works and talks about the need for them. Is it possible we've gotten this wrong?

Jesus Speaks About Works to Convict Us of Sin

Jesus speaks to his followers in the Beatitudes. He speaks about what it means to live as a forgiven child of God who knows that this world has everything backwards. He says,

Matthew 5:17-20—*"Do not think that I have come to abolish the Law or the Prophets; I have not come to abolish them but to fulfill them. I tell you the truth, until heaven and earth disappear, not the smallest letter, not the least stroke of a pen, will by any means disappear from the Law until everything is accomplished. Anyone who breaks one of the least of these commandments and teaches others to do the same will be called least in the kingdom of heaven, but whoever practices* *and teaches these commands will be called great in the kingdom of heaven. For I tell you that unless your righteousness surpasses that of the Pharisees and the teachers of the law, you will certainly not enter the kingdom of heaven."*

Jesus says that greatness in heaven is found in keeping the commandments! More than that, he says that unless your righteousness (holiness) is greater than that of the holiest-seeming people of Jesus' day, you won't enter heaven. And as you read through the rest of what Jesus has to say, he just drives home the point more. Calling your brother a fool puts you in the dangers of hellfire.[16] Looking at a woman lustfully makes you guilty of adultery.[17]

Words like that should make the name-calling Christian man shake with fear! And not just him. Words like that should make a lusting man or woman shake with fear! If even the Pharisees,[18] who dedicated their lives to observing God's laws, were not righteous enough, then who is?

And that's exactly Jesus' point. No one is righteous enough to enter heaven. We all deserve hell. It sounds like a shocking statement—until you spend time truly thinking about it. To be in heaven is to stand in the presence of a holy God who is completely separate from sin. (After all, how could a holy God tolerate sin?) To be in heaven is to be in the presence of perfect love, perfect joy, and perfect peace that last an eternity. Should even the kindest and most loving human be arrogant enough to say, "Yes! I've earned that kind of eternal reward! God should be honored to have me in his presence!"? Would even the most loving of us dare to say that we're not guilty of sins that God hates?

That's one of the reasons Jesus speaks of good works and human righteousness. He wants us to know that God's standard of righteousness is far higher than we could ever reach. Do you think you're

---

[16] Matthew 5:22.

[17] Matthew 5:28.

[18] The Pharisees were a religious sect in Christ's day. They sought to observe every law from the Old Testament so zealously that they added hundreds of their own laws and their own regulations governing every part of their daily lives.

"good enough" to earn an eternity with God in heaven? Then consider Jesus' words carefully. If you're honest with them—and honest with yourself—you'll realize that you aren't good enough. You need more than you're able to give. You need a Savior.

And you have one.

Jesus Boldly Proclaims That Salvation Is by Grace

Jesus said that to earn heaven our righteousness would need to surpass that of the most seemingly religious leaders of his day. But there's another way to enter heaven—one that has nothing to do with our earning or deserving it. It was fitting, then, that Jesus spoke the following words to the religious leaders!

> **Matthew 21:31,32**—*Jesus said to them, "I tell you the truth, the tax collectors and the prostitutes are entering the kingdom of God ahead of you. For John came to you to show you the way of righteousness, and you did not believe him, but the tax collectors and the prostitutes did. And even after you saw this, you did not repent and believe him."*

If only the most perfect people will be in heaven, who can you expect to find there? The whores. The cheats. If those words surprise you, then you understand what Jesus says. Righteousness isn't found in how good we are; we just can't be good enough. Who would understand that better than a prostitute or tax collector?[19] And Jesus says, "Do you want to go to heaven? Then follow the prostitutes! Realize your sinfulness, just as they did. Turn to me for forgiveness, just as they did." What a bold statement of how far God's grace must reach! How could those sinners enter heaven?

> **John 3:16**—*"God so loved the world that he gave his one and only Son, that whoever believes in him shall not perish but have eternal life."*

---

[19] The tax collectors in Jesus' day were notoriously corrupt. It was by design; the Roman system of "tax farming" encouraged corruption. Tax collectors *needed* to be corrupt and prey on their people to make a living, and they were hated and seen as traitors for doing so.

We know those words so well that it's easy to let our eyes pass over them without thinking about what they really mean. Don't. Jesus says that God loves "the world." Not "religious people." Not "those who do the best they can." "The world." The world is filled with child abusers, murderers, drug dealers, men who beat their wives, and mothers who abandon their children. And God looks at the world full of people who've broken every last rule and law he's ever given, people who've hurt (and even killed!) his own children, and he loves them. This is grace. This is God's love.

It reaches even the worst of the worst.

Luke 23:43—*Jesus answered him, "I tell you the truth, today you will be with me in paradise."*

A man was dying on the cross next to Jesus. He deserved to be there. It sounds like a heartless statement, but the man himself admitted it.[20] Who knows what twists and turns his life had taken? The people he'd wronged. The goods he'd stolen. The blood he'd shed. He had no righteousness of his own—certainly nothing that would atone for his life of wickedness. He couldn't give; he could only receive.

That was good. Jesus was there to give. And he gave that sinner a promise of paradise.

At some point over the years, the church decided to refer to that man as "Dismas." That Latin name is where we get our English word *dismal*. But it's not a sad name. In Latin it means "sunset." Do you see the connection? As that wicked criminal who deserved a cross watched the sun set, he knew he would die soon. He knew his sins earned that, and far worse. But he also knew that Jesus had given him a promise that before the sun set below the horizon that day, he would be standing with his Savior in heaven. Free from pain. Free from guilt. Face-to-face with a God who loved even him. Has anyone ever seen a more beautiful sunset than he?

Jesus speaks about good works. He tells us what it takes to earn heaven. It's more than we can give, so he gives it to us. He makes sure

---

[20] The dying criminal said, "We are punished justly, for we are getting what our deeds deserve" (Luke 23:41).

we can't put any confidence in our own righteousness, then he shows us the righteousness he's earned for us.

It's a righteousness that changes us.

Jesus Speaks About Works to Guide Our Christian Living

Jesus told a parable to help us understand the change grace works in us:

Matthew 25:14-30—*"Again, it will be like a man going on a journey, who called his servants and entrusted his property to them. To one he gave five talents of money, to another two talents, and to another one talent, each according to his ability. Then he went on his journey. The man who had received the five talents went at once and put his money to work and gained five more. So also, the one with the two talents gained two more. But the man who had received the one talent went off, dug a hole in the ground and hid his master's money. After a long time the master of those servants returned and settled accounts with them. The man who had received the five talents brought the other five. 'Master,' he said, 'you entrusted me with five talents. See, I have gained five more.' His master replied, 'Well done, good and faithful servant! You have been faithful with a few things; I will put you in charge of many things. Come and share your master's happiness!' The man with the two talents also came. 'Master,' he said, 'you entrusted me with two talents; see, I have gained two more.' His master replied, 'Well done, good and faithful servant! You have been faithful with a few things; I will put you in charge of many things. Come and share your master's happiness!' Then the man who had received the one talent came. 'Master,' he said, 'I knew that you are a hard man, harvesting where you have not sown and gathering where you have not scattered seed. So I was afraid and went out and hid your talent in the ground. See, here is what belongs to you.' His master replied, 'You wicked, lazy servant! So you knew that I harvest where I have not sown and gather where I have not scattered seed? Well then, you should have put my money on deposit with the bankers, so that when I returned I would have received it back with interest. Take the talent* *from him and give it to the one who has the ten talents. For everyone who has will be given more, and he will have an abundance. Whoever does not have, even what he has will be taken from him. And throw that worthless servant outside, into the darkness, where there will be weeping and gnashing of teeth.'"*

A new Christian walked out of church after hearing a sermon on Matthew chapter 25. He looked at the pastor and said, "I have to tell you, that one confused me. I thought the master was the villain of the story. But he's supposed to show us what God is like?"

It's easy to see why the new Christian struggled with that. The master gives his servants money to work with while he's off traveling (he doesn't even give them each the same amount!). At first glance, he only seems interested in getting returns on his investments. By his own admission, he seems to agree with the servant who views him as a "hard man." When that worker underperforms, he punishes him.

But look carefully at the master's reaction to the servants who worked faithfully. It's not, "Wonderful! More money for me!" Rather, he says, "Come and share your master's happiness." His goal isn't lining his pockets; it's blessing his people.

Jesus' words ask the believer, "How do you see God?" Seeing him as an angry master who uses the threat of punishment is enough to get us to do some good things, at least outwardly. That might scare us away from cheating on our spouses or murdering our neighbors. But it's not enough to change our hearts. As long as we see God that way, our hearts will always be silently saying, "I know that you are a hard man. . . ." And our talents will be hidden in the ground. Seeing God as the angry master means God's love will bear no fruit in our lives. At the beginning of this chapter, you read about a "Christian" man who seemed to have no fear of his sin. When we start to act like that man, these words of Jesus' parable speak volumes to us. A person content to live in his or her sins does not understand God's grace. And anyone who doesn't understand God's grace has every reason to expect to be thrown into the darkness. They don't truly know God.

But this is who God is: He's a God who saves us by the life and death of his own Son—fully, completely, freely. He's a God who wants us to share in his happiness—not just the happiness of standing with him in heaven but the joy that comes from truly loving people, serving them as Christ served us, and living lives that have a purpose which will echo through eternity. See God this way; his love yields a harvest in our lives.

Jesus speaks of good works. The whole Bible speaks about good works and the need for us to do them. But it's not about doing enough or being good enough for God. Remember, "unless your righteousness surpasses that of the Pharisees"?

Jesus has something to say to the Christian man who seems to have no fear of his sin and the non-Christian woman who dedicates her life to serving others. His words remind both of them and all of us that no matter how hard we strive, we don't deserve heaven with God. When we see that, his words of free grace tell us of a God who has boundless love and forgiveness for a dying criminal, a wicked world, and each of us. Don't you see what God is most interested in? It's not our works. It's our salvation. So go and serve him with joy!

"Unless You Hate Your Father and Mother . . ."

Love matters to Jesus. He's all about it. When Jesus speaks about love, he speaks about love that has more beauty, more commitment, and more selflessness than anything the world knows by nature.

"Love the Lord your God with all your heart and with all your soul and with all your mind. . . . Love your neighbor as yourself."[21]

"Greater love has no one than this, that he lay down his life for his friends."[22]

"God so loved the world that he gave his one and only Son."[23]

"I tell you: Love your enemies."[24]

When we talk about love, we barely scratch the surface. We say we love our children but get irritated when they inconvenience our lives. We say we love our spouses, but if we feel unhappy long enough, we'll set aside our marriage promises for someone else. We talk about loving all people, but our streets are filled with people in need and we're often filled with excuses not to help them. We fumble around with the most precious thing.

Jesus doesn't. He talks about love that consumes and controls everything inside of us. He talks about love that doesn't hesitate to face torture to save one's friends, love that doesn't hesitate to face death to save one's enemies. Jesus talks about love in a way that not only wins our hearts but makes us want to share his words with our friends, our families—anyone who will listen.

But Jesus also talks about hate. In fact, he talks about hating our friends and families.

---

[21] Matthew 22:37,39.

[22] John 15:13.

[23] John 3:16.

[24] Matthew 5:44.

Hard Sayings of Jesus

Even When Jesus Talks About Hate, His Goal Is Still Love

Luke 14:25,26—*Large crowds were traveling with Jesus, and turning to them he said: "If anyone comes to me and does not hate his father and mother, his wife and children, his brothers and sisters—yes, even his own life—he cannot be my disciple."*

It's not a poor English translation; Jesus calls us to *hate*. And not just to hate someone (our enemies? those who oppose the gospel?) but to hate our parents, our spouses, our children—even ourselves. And if we don't? Jesus says we can't be his disciples.

These are hard words! Nothing can make them easy for us, but paying attention to the context can at least help us understand why Jesus spoke them.

Jesus had just told a story about a great banquet. A man sent out his servant to let all his guests know: *Everything is ready!* But they didn't come. They had their reasons. One wanted to look in on his real estate investment. Another wanted to try out his new teams of oxen. Another was a newlywed.

But the man wanted his blessings to be enjoyed, so he sent his invitation far and wide. His servant invited anyone and everyone who would hear and come. The man wanted his house full and his banquet to be enjoyed. The only ones who didn't get a taste were the ones who loved other things more.

Jesus doesn't want us to miss out on the blessings he won for us. And he doesn't want us to pursue them without considering the cost. Right after calling us to hate those closest to us, he speaks of a man who started building a tower without considering if he was able to pay the cost to complete it.

God loves us fully and completely. His love holds nothing back, not even his own Son. That love calls for our complete commitment to him. We cannot truly love God if we place anyone or anything before him. He wants us to understand that, so we don't end up like guests who didn't make the banquet or a bankrupt man who wept in the shadow of a half-built tower for which he could not pay. He speaks of hating others because he doesn't want us to miss out on his love.

Is the only way to avoid that fate to hate the people closest to us? It doesn't seem possible. After all, this is the same Jesus who tells us to love our enemies. He certainly wants us to love our dear ones too.

Jesus spoke on this same point another time, which St. Matthew recorded for us. These words help bring a bit more understanding.

Matthew 10:34-39—*"Do not suppose that I have come to bring peace to the earth. I did not come to bring peace, but a sword. For I have come to turn 'a man against his father, a daughter against her mother, a daughter-in-law against her mother-in-law—a man's enemies will be the members of his own household.' Anyone who loves his father or mother more than me is not worthy of me; anyone who loves his son or daughter more than me is not worthy of me; and anyone who does not take his cross and follow me is not worthy of me. Whoever finds his life will lose it, and whoever loses his life for my sake will find it."*

These words don't start off any easier. Jesus recognizes that when we put God first and hold to his truth, it can cause problems in our earthly relationships. Sometimes there's no way around that; it's simply part of the cost of following the Savior who preaches a message contrary to this world's natural thinking.

But notice the difference this time. Rather than telling us to hate those closest to us, Jesus simply calls us not to love them more than we love God. He doesn't want our love for them to be so great that we'd be willing to sacrifice any part of our relationship with God for them. And he doesn't just want that for *his* glory. He wants us to keep him first because he is the only source of true love and the only way to salvation. How many times has someone let his or her faith become less important, little by little, to avoid conflict with or have more time for the person he or she loves? How many times have angels wept over people who were trading God's eternal love for something far briefer and dimmer?

So does this mean that Jesus' call to hate our families is simply an exaggeration? a very bold way of saying, "Don't love them more than me"? It's best to start by trying to understand how God looks at us. It's not simple. He says he hates us. He hates us so much for our sins that he would damn us to hell for them. Yet, at the same time, he loves us—every last sinner—more than we could imagine.

And that's what he calls believers to do too. It's a godly thing for believers to hate those who oppose God.[25] The Bible has countless examples of God's people doing so. Read the letters of Peter and Paul in the New Testament, and consider the hatred they show toward those who would teach false doctrines that would lead people to hell. But Jesus calls us to love all people too. God calls us to "do good to all people,"[26] to love our enemies,[27] to love others the same way that he loves us.[28] He calls us to hate according to sin and to love empowered by grace.

That even applies to our loved ones. If someone in our lives is causing a stumbling block in our faith, mocking us for our faith, and just taking us away from God by inches, God says, "Hate that. Hate them." God does. He hates anyone or anything that would threaten to take us from a perfect eternity in heaven with him and lead his redeemed children to hell. But remember, he doesn't stop there. At the same time, he says, "Love them." Love them so much that you'll warn them. Love them so much that you'll share your faith with them all the more. Love them so much that you'll forgive them.

It's understandable that the God who knows he's our only way of salvation wants to be first in our lives. It's just not easy. I love my daughter as I walk her to school; my son is my world as I lay him down to sleep; my wife is my waking and my sleeping. Jesus doesn't want to stop that; he wants to make it everything it can be. When we love Jesus first and best, that doesn't diminish those other loves; it enriches them. I won't just love my children and my wife for the joy they bring me. I will love them because I know how much they matter to my Savior. I won't just give them what they need for 18 years or 80; every day I'll seek to help them

---

[25] See Psalm 31:6 for one example.
[26] Galatians 6:10.
[27] Matthew 5:44.
[28] John 13:34.

grow in a love that will last forever. That's what Jesus wants us to have.

Even when it comes at a cost.

Holding to God's Love Means Letting Go

Mark 9:43-48—*"If your hand causes you to sin, cut it off. It is better for you to enter life maimed than with two hands to go into hell, where the fire never goes out. And if your foot causes you to sin, cut it off. It is better for you to enter life crippled than to have two feet and be thrown into hell. And if your eye causes you to sin, pluck it out. It is better for you to enter the kingdom of God with one eye than to have two eyes and be thrown into hell, where 'their worm does not die, and the fire is not quenched.'"*

It sounds like something out of a horror movie. Cutting off your own hand or foot? Plucking out your eye? If you think that Jesus means this in a literal way, consider what that would look like. Even if the world was filled with footless, handless, eyeless people, it would still be a world filled with sinners. In chapter 4 we looked at Jesus' words, that our sinfulness does not come from the food we eat—well neither does our sin come from our hands, feet, or eyes. It comes from our hearts, our souls. We can't cut it out.

Jesus' point shines through in verse 47: "It is better for you to enter the kingdom of God with one eye than to have two eyes and be thrown into hell." God wants us to hold on to his love. He wants us to hold on to our forgiveness. He wants us to hold on to heaven. And that means letting go of anything that would get in the way.

Take those words to heart. God loves you. He's freed you from your sins and given you a home in heaven. What are you holding on to that will get in the way of that? A relationship with pornography that wars against your soul?[29] A vengeful hatred for someone who took advantage of you or abused you?[30] Friends who make it clear

---

[29] 1 Peter 2:11.
[30] 1 John 3:15.

they don't have any time for your faith and who don't want you to show it when you're around them?[31] A job that brings you so much earthly fulfillment and peace but takes you away from time in God's Word at home or with believers at church?[32] Look carefully at the trade you're making. Is it at work? with your budget? in your relationships? None of those things is worth risking the loss of heaven. Don't make excuses. Don't procrastinate. Grab a knife. Do some surgery. Hold to God's love, even if it means letting go of something else. It seems terrifying—what surgery doesn't?—but like Jesus said, "It is better for you to enter the kingdom of God." Then you're holding on to something worthwhile.

Sometime in the next week or so, talk to someone about love, and not just anyone either. Find someone who's been married for decades and knows what it's like to see someone through thick and thin, through good times and bad—for better or for worse. Ask that person to tell you what love means to him or her. You likely won't hear stories about flowers and poems and boxes of chocolate. Instead, you might hear about forgiveness after betrayal, unspeakable sacrifice, and nights spent by hospital beds. It might not always be pretty, but as you listen, you'll likely notice that there's no regret in the voice of the one speaking. This person knows that the love he or she has shared is worth it and this person would never let it go.

"God so loved the world. . . ." Dear believer, hold this truth tightly.

---

[31] 1 Corinthians 15:33.
[32] John 15:5; Exodus 20:8.

"Be as Shrewd as Snakes"

Machiavelli knew that evil acts were wrong, but he also knew they could serve a good purpose. That's the argument the Italian philosopher put forward in his work *The Prince* almost five hundred years ago. He praised virtue and justice but argued that sometimes a few acts of evil could help avoid much greater problems. Of course murder is wrong, but if a new king murdering a few dozen of his enemies would spare a nation from decades of war, isn't that a good thing? Isn't sacrificing the lives of a few a lesser evil than letting hundreds or thousands die?

He never used the exact words, but Machiavelli's idea has been described as "the ends justify the means." As long as the goal you're pursuing is good, a little evil along the way can be tolerated. It makes sense. What good are moral arguments about preserving life if refusing to kill a few means the death of so many more? If telling a few lies helps accomplish a noble goal, isn't that a good thing?

"I am the way and the truth and the life,"[33] Jesus said. God's Son came into a world that finds virtue in lies and wisdom in wickedness, but he spoke and lived pure truth. And he calls us to do the same. Consider the following:

> **2 Corinthians 4:2**—*We have renounced secret and shameful ways; we do not use deception, nor do we distort the word of God. On the contrary, by setting forth the truth plainly we commend ourselves to every man's conscience in the sight of God.*

> **Matthew 5:37**—*"Simply let your 'Yes' be 'Yes,' and your 'No,' 'No'; anything beyond this comes from the evil one."*

> **2 Corinthians 1:12**—*Now this is our boast: Our conscience testifies that we have conducted ourselves in the world, and especially in our relations with you, in the holiness and sincerity that are from God.*

---

[33] John 14:6.

We have done so not according to worldly wisdom but according to God's grace.

Colossians 3:9,10—*Do not lie to each other, since you have taken off your old self with its practices and have put on the new self, which is being renewed in knowledge in the image of its Creator.*

The Christian's goal is to share eternal life with people, to save souls for eternity. If a little lie, a half-truth, or a small deception would help accomplish that, shouldn't we do it? If we know a truth of Scripture is at odds with the culture we're working in, doesn't it make sense to downplay that truth? If hiding our faith avoids persecution, isn't it wise to do so? No! God says we're to be honest, not because it's wise but because we follow the One who *is* truth. We should always be honest and open.

Right?

Jesus Calls His People to Be Shrewd

Matthew 10:16—*"I am sending you out like sheep among wolves. Therefore be as shrewd as snakes and as innocent as doves."*

Shrewdness is more than wisdom. It's often associated with being *cunning* or *tricky*. If you're shrewd, you are able to size up a situation and use everything to your advantage to achieve your goal. And as if that weren't problematic enough, Jesus uses snakes as his point of comparison. Snakes have never been seen as a symbol of honesty (especially in Scripture!). How could any believer hear those words and not hear an echo of the fall into sin: "Now the serpent was more crafty than any of the wild animals"?[34] It's easy to understand how people could see Jesus' advice as being the same as Machiavelli's: *The ends justify the means.*

Shrewdness isn't the same as wickedness. Jesus made that clear by immediately calling us to be "as innocent as doves." He isn't commanding us to sin. But withholding portions of the truth—even

---

[34]Genesis 3:1.

sometimes intentionally misleading someone—isn't the same as malicious lying. That's a difficult concept. Ask many Christians to name as many of the Ten Commandments as they can and you'll likely hear, "Do not lie," from most of them. (For the record, that isn't one of the commandments.) How does that fit with the God who *is* truth and calls us to speak in truth?

Perhaps a few biblical examples can help show what *shrewdness* looks like:

- "[Solomon] then gave an order: 'Cut the living child in two and give half to one and half to the other'" (I Kings 3:25). Solomon's "wise ruling" is famous. Two women shared a home. Both had young sons. After one son died in the middle of the night and the deceased child's mother switched the children, the women brought the matter to the wise king to determine whose son the living boy truly was. Solomon had no intention of slaughtering the surviving boy. His goal was the truth. He understood the nature of a loving parent. To reveal the truth, he proposed a course of action with which he didn't intend to follow through. Was he deceitful? He was shrewd.

- "Do not rebuke a mocker or he will hate you; rebuke a wise man and he will love you" (Proverbs 9:8). God calls us to confront sin. He tells his people to "correct, rebuke and encourage"[35] one another. But this practical advice from Proverbs adds the instruction, ". . . but not all the time. Just at the right time." What's the goal of a rebuke? It's to correct someone who will listen. Solomon reminds us that some people simply won't take a rebuke; they're mockers. That's true of some people; that's likely true of all of us at some point in our lives. Sometimes a needed rebuke will simply not be heard. Sometimes it's best to wait until the time when the person is more prepared to hear it. That's not ignoring sin; it's being shrewd.

- "As [the two disciples on the way to Emmaus] talked and discussed these things with each other, Jesus himself came

---

[35] 2 Timothy 4:2.

up and walked along with them; but they were kept from recognizing him. As they approached the village to which they were going, Jesus acted as if he were going farther" (Luke 24:15,16,28). There was nothing those disciples wanted more than to see their Savior alive again. But it seems Jesus himself was the one who kept them from recognizing him. A deception? If that specific instance wasn't, there was certainly some acting going on when the disciples reached their destination and Jesus gave the impression that he intended to go farther. He had no such intent. But Jesus' goal wasn't to convince them of a falsehood. It was to open their eyes to the truth. Instead of simply revealing himself to them, he wanted first to open the Scriptures to them so they could have real comfort and confidence even after Jesus ascended and they couldn't see him anymore. He wasn't seeking to con them. He was being shrewd.

Jesus doesn't want his people to be malicious liars. He calls us to be as innocent as doves, even when we're being shrewd. It may strike our ears a little odd to hear that not all deception is sinful, but we're perhaps more aware of that than we think! Benevolent deception can be a very good teaching tool. A teacher might lead her students down the path toward a wrong answer to help them recognize her errors and argue for the right conclusion. Parents hide some financial difficulties or marriage problems from their children because they're not old enough to deal with them. Read again the account of Genesis chapter 3. The serpent was not the only cunning one. God asked Adam where he was—not because God didn't know but because he wanted to give Adam a chance to come back to him. He asked Adam and Eve what they had done—not because he didn't know about their sin but because he wanted them to be able to confess to him. That kind of deception isn't wickedness; it's a tool used to bring people to the truth.

Christians are to be shrewd as they pursue their goal of sharing the truth. When missionaries spread the gospel in lands where evangelism is illegal, they often don't give full disclosure to the hostile government about the nature of their work. Parents might act like they don't know who dented the car so that their child might learn to confess and be forgiven. That's a far cry from using outright wickedness to pursue whatever goal we want, but we're right to struggle with the applications at times. If you ever wrestle with that, let both parts of Jesus' guidance stand: Do be shrewd. Yet remember, *as innocent as doves.*

Shrewd Stewards Pursue a Heavenly Goal

Perhaps *innocent* isn't the first word that comes to mind when we hear about the shrewd manager in Jesus' parable.

> **Luke 16:1-9**—*Jesus told his disciples: "There was a rich man whose manager was accused of wasting his possessions. So he called him in and asked him, 'What is this I hear about you? Give an account of your management, because you cannot be manager any longer.' The manager said to himself, 'What shall I do now? My master is taking away my job. I'm not strong enough to dig, and I'm ashamed to beg— I know what I'll do so that, when I lose my job here, people will welcome me into their houses.' So he called in each one of his master's debtors. He asked the first, 'How much do you owe my master?' 'Eight hundred gallons of olive oil,' he replied. The manager told him, 'Take your bill, sit down quickly, and make it four hundred.' Then he asked the second, 'And how much do you owe?' 'A thousand bushels of wheat,' he replied. He told him, 'Take your bill and make it eight hundred.' The master commended the dishonest manager because he had acted shrewdly. For the people of this world are more shrewd in dealing with their own kind than are the people of the light. I tell you, use worldly wealth to gain friends for yourselves, so that when it is gone, you will be welcomed into eternal dwellings."*

The guy was a crook. His actions weren't illegal, but they were certainly immoral. Since he knew he was going to be fired, he abused his position as the manager of his master's finances to make sure he'd have friends waiting for him once he lost his position. It was scheming, underhanded, and manipulative. And Jesus says, "Be like him."

A parable is an illustration. Think of it as a metaphor. Every metaphor has a point of comparison. (If someone says, "Your wife is a real gem," they mean she's a priceless treasure. They don't mean she's hard and shiny like a gemstone.) When you read the parable of the shrewd manager, don't think Jesus is encouraging us to be underhanded and greedy.

Christ himself tells us the lesson we should learn from this parable. There are a few translation difficulties in this section. While the NIV 1984 was quoted here, consider the New King James Version's translation of verse 9: "I say to you, make friends for yourselves by unrighteous mammon,[36] that when you fail, they may receive you into an everlasting home." Notice two differences from the NIV 1984 translation:

1. Jesus isn't focusing us on the day when our money runs out (or "fails"); he's directing us to consider what happens when we "fail" (that is, pass away).
2. The focus isn't on *us being welcomed* into our heavenly home. It's on the "they"—that is, the friends we make—being there in heaven to welcome us.

The shrewd manager's goal was a selfish and worldly one. He simply wanted a comfortable life with friends to provide for him. He used everything at his disposal to achieve his goal. That's the point of comparison Jesus is making. That's shrewdness. He wants us to have the same insightfulness and mindfulness as we pursue our goal as believers. That goal isn't a comfortable life with plenty of friends; it's sharing Jesus with as many people as we can so that they can stand in heaven with us one day. It's a heavenly goal that Jesus wants us to pursue with no less wisdom than people pursue their earthly goals.

And he includes a mild rebuke for us to take to heart: "The people of this world are more shrewd in dealing with their own kind than are the people of the light" (Luke 16:8). The world is filled with people who shrewdly use their time, their resources, and their relationships to get ahead at work, to craft the lifestyle they want, to fill their lives with friends, or to prepare a wonderful retirement.

---

[36] "Mammon" is an English translation of the Greek word that Luke recorded. It includes "money" but has a wider meaning than that. It also includes all our physical possessions and material "stuff."

Those are their goals, and they pursue them shrewdly. Christian, do the same. Consider all the resources God has given to you. Remember your goal of sharing the gospel with other sinners. Pursue it shrewdly. Use everything at your disposal to bring it about.

What does that look like? Perhaps it means making friends with new neighbors simply in the hopes of being able to share your Savior with them or inviting them to church. A congregation might put this into action by opening a preschool, not just with the goal of educating young minds but with the goal of sharing salvation with young souls. A church body might respond to a humanitarian crisis with hundreds of thousands of dollars' worth of aid, not because their chief goal is rebuilding earthquake-devastated homes but because they want to rebuild broken relationships with God. We use earthly wealth to make friends for ourselves because we remember our goal: when our lives pass away, we want to open our eyes and see those people we befriended standing at Jesus' side in heaven.

Jesus is not Machiavelli. He doesn't tell us to use whatever means necessary to achieve our goals. He doesn't tell us to use wickedness for the sake of righteousness. The believer doesn't act like scheming royalty, willing to be ruthless to protect his or her own rule.

Jesus is the Way, the Truth, and the Life. He calls us to remember our goals as we look at all of the resources that he's placed into our hands. He tells us to be shrewd, seizing every opportunity to accomplish his work. When that happens, the believer doesn't look like a royalty. The believer looks like a dove—with the shrewdness of a snake.

11

Pearls Before Swine and Bread to Dogs

Matthew 7:1—*"Do not judge, or you too will be judged."*

It's one of the most quoted Bible passages in the world.

If you're reading this book, maybe that catches you off guard. After all, ask a Christian for his or her favorite Bible passage and you might expect something like "God so loved the world that he gave his one and only Son"[37] or "I can do everything through him who gives me strength."[38] And those still are some of the most quoted passages among believers.

But Jesus' words against judging form one of the most quoted passages among those who don't identify as Christians. Perhaps that *doesn't* catch you off guard after all. Many Christians have had the experience of trying to correct a sinning friend with some words of Jesus, only to have more of Jesus' words thrown back at them: *"Do not judge! Your God is the one who tells you not to judge me, so stop talking to me about sin!"* Checkmate.

In reality, Jesus does talk about judging . . . a lot. He speaks of the way he'll come to judge the world.[39] He tells the disciples that they will sit in judgment over the 12 tribes of Israel on the Last Day.[40] Every time he tells us to watch out for false prophets or to flee from sinful desires,[41] Jesus is telling us to make a judgment.

So what does he mean when he says, "Do not judge, or you too will be judged"?

---

[37] John 3:16.

[38] Philippians 4:13. As an interesting side note, in recent years a number of surveys have identified this passage as the one most frequently quoted and shared, at least in online social media. One wonders if this is a reflection of what many see as American Christianity's shift of emphasis from *justification* to *sanctification*.

[39] Matthew 25:31ff is just one example.

[40] Matthew 19:28.

[41] Matthew 7:15.

Jesus Forbids Hypocritical Judgment

As always, it's important to look at Jesus' words in context.

Matthew 7:1-5—*"Do not judge, or you too will be judged. For in the same way you judge others, you will be judged, and with the measure you use, it will be measured to you. Why do you look at the speck of sawdust in your brother's eye and pay no attention to the plank in your own eye? How can you say to your brother, 'Let me take the speck out of your eye,' when all the time there is a plank in your own eye? You hypocrite, first take the plank out of your own eye, and then you will see clearly to remove the speck from your brother's eye."*

How we judge others is a reflection of what we believe. If we believe that God deals with us with mercy and forgiveness and that his true goal isn't to punish sinners but to turn them from their ways so that they might live, then we'll deal with people in that same way. Our goal will be to show them mercy. When we talk about right and wrong, it will be with the goal of turning them from their sins so that they can live in God's forgiveness.

And the opposite is true too. If our goal is simply to judge others by the letter of the law, we're showing that is how we believe God works: not with grace, simply with the law. And if we don't believe in grace, we won't receive it either.

For a believer, that kind of judging is hypocritical! It ignores our sin, which God freely forgives, and focuses on the sins of others. The way Jesus describes it is almost laughable: Can you picture how foolish it would look for a man with a two-by-four sticking out of his eye to be focused on the speck of sawdust in someone else's eye?

That's the kind of foolish judgment that comes naturally to us. It's a judgment that ignores our own sins because it feels empowering and self-justifying to focus on the sins of others. It springs from a heart that's convinced (even if we would never say it out loud!): *I am better than you.* That judging is hypocritical. It's laughable. It's sinful. Jesus condemns that judging.

But he doesn't condemn all judging. You can see that in the very next words he speaks.

Matthew 7:5,6—*"You hypocrite, first take the plank out of your own eye, and then you will see clearly to remove the speck from your brother's eye. Do not give dogs what is sacred; do not throw your pearls to pigs. If you do, they may trample them under their feet, and then turn and tear you to pieces."*

Jesus' words demand judgment from us—and no light or easy judgment at that! By telling us not to "give dogs what is sacred" or "throw your pearls to pigs," he's telling us that, at times, we need to make the judgment that if we speak God's Word to someone who's made it clear that they have no use or respect for it, we're doing no good. In fact, we're just allowing them to dishonor God's Word and giving them more reasons to attack us.

He's also calling us to view some people as "dogs" or "pigs."

It sounds horribly disrespectful, doesn't it? Perhaps that's why Jesus spoke these words immediately after his warning against hypocritical judgment. If we're going to judge rightly, we need to remember who we are: forgiven sinners. We have plenty of sins of our own and are only forgiven by God's grace. God showed love for us when we had done nothing to deserve it.

We need to show that love to others—Jesus isn't telling us anything that contradicts that. He's telling us what to do when people insist on rejecting that love. If someone repeatedly rejects God's warnings against sin, rejects his forgiveness, and mocks what he has to say, then God says putting his Word in front of that person again would be as foolish as giving sacred things to a dog or pearls to a pig.

God did it. He sent Moses with a message for Pharaoh. Through Moses' words, God warned Pharaoh repeatedly to call him back from sin. Pharaoh stubbornly hardened his heart again and again—for a while. Then God himself stepped in and hardened Pharaoh's heart.[42] God wouldn't have his sacred love thrown to a dog. He even did this with his own people. He sent prophet after prophet to the northern tribes of Israel. The Israelites rejected the prophets, mocked them, and killed them. So God stopped sending them. Instead, he sent the

---

[42] Exodus 9:12.

Assyrian army to break the Israelites' nation and carry the people away to a land where they would not hear God's Word. God is patient and loving, but he doesn't throw his pearls to pigs forever.

And we aren't to do that either. How do you make that judgment? Jesus tells you how. You can only make that judgment as someone who knows your own sinfulness and who wants to show someone else mercy. You make the judgment as someone whose *goal* isn't to show others that you're better than they are but as someone whose goal is to bring people to know the same gracious God that you've come to know. And if—and only if—a person repeatedly rejects the grace and mercy of God, you might make the difficult judgment that God calls us to make at times. We pray for God to bring the day when he would change that person's heart and for him to give you a chance to share the Word with this person again. That's God's true goal, and it's our goal too.

But when Jesus spoke, it didn't always look like such a godly goal.

Even When Jesus Seems to Look Down on Us, He's Calling Us to Look Up to His Promises

Matthew 15:22-28—*A Canaanite woman from that vicinity came to him, crying out, "Lord, Son of David, have mercy on me! My daughter is suffering terribly from demon-possession." Jesus did not answer a word. So his disciples came to him and urged him, "Send her away, for she keeps crying out after us." He answered, "I was sent only to the lost sheep of Israel." The woman came and knelt before him. "Lord, help me!" she said. He replied, "It is not right to take the children's bread and toss it to their dogs." "Yes, Lord," she said, "but even the dogs eat the crumbs that fall from their masters' table." Then Jesus answered, "Woman, you have great faith! Your request is granted." And her daughter was healed from that very hour.*

It's hard not to grimace when you read those words. We can understand Jesus' point when he talks about someone who repeatedly rejects God's grace and squanders his mercy as a *dog*. But this was a mother whose daughter was suffering. She came to Jesus seeking his help, believing that he really was someone who had power and mercy. That's what God wants, isn't it? He wants people who look to him for mercy and who believe that he has the power and love to help us. And Jesus calls her a dog.

There's some Bible history that's important to understand. Matthew tells us that she was a "Canaanite woman." She wasn't an Israelite. She was a descendant of those tribes that had lived in the Promised Land until the Israelites arrived. The Lord told the Israelites to wipe them out, but they didn't. The Canaanites were generally pagan. This woman had at least heard some basic truths about Jesus, but still, she was a Canaanite. Jesus came to be the Savior of the world, but his earthly ministry was focused on revealing himself to the Jewish people.

This woman understood that. And as hard as Jesus' words are for us to read, they also recognize the situation. Translators have long drawn attention to the fact that the word Jesus used for "dog" doesn't mean anything like "street cur" or "mongrel." It means something more like "house dog." That may seem like a small comfort, but Martin Luther rightly observed how Christ's words would have been heard by the woman: "Yet all those trials of her faith sounded more like no than yes; but there was more yea in them than nay; aye, there is only yes in them, but it is very deep and very concealed, while there appears to be nothing but no."[43]

Don't think for a minute that Jesus' words were meant to show disrespect to that woman or to send her away without his aid and mercy. Listen to how the whole affair ended: "Woman, you have great faith!" Jesus' words were hard, but he spoke them for a purpose. Consider the effect of his words that day. To the disciples, this woman wasn't worthy of Jesus' aid. She wasn't one of them. She wasn't of the people of Israel. To them, she was a distraction and a bother. Jesus taught them a lesson that day. Our connection to God and his mercy doesn't depend on who we are or where we come from.

---

[43] *The Complete Sermons of Martin Luther*, Vol II (Grand Rapids: Baker Book House, 2000), p. 152.

It's found in clinging to God's promises. It wasn't to the disciples but to this Canaanite, this woman, this "dog," that Jesus said, "You have great faith!" And there's no doubt Jesus' words tested this woman that day too. Clinging to God's promises is hard sometimes. Sometimes it feels as though God isn't listening or answering. But hold to his promises and you won't be disappointed.

Remember that when you feel like this Canaanite woman. You aren't the first one to struggle with Jesus' answers (or lack of answers) to prayer. Maybe you read this account and think, "I know exactly what she felt like. I was hurting so much, and I went to Jesus for help. I believed he could help me. But he didn't. I felt like I didn't matter to him." It's true: God doesn't always answer us in the way we would want or expect; there are plenty of daughters who don't get healed despite their mothers' earnest prayers. Sometimes God leads us through the troubles to help us rely on his grace even more. Sometimes he's achieving a purpose we just won't be aware of before heaven.

But if you feel like that woman, God wants you to be like that woman. Keep going back to his promises. Read your Bible. Gather around his Word with other Christians. When you do that, you aren't a dog or a swine—even if you feel like a house pet!—but you are a child of God.

12 "Why Have You Forsaken Me?"

In the Bible, God recorded seven different statements that Jesus spoke from the cross. They aren't hard to understand. Many Christians are used to hearing them read every year on Good Friday.[44] Even if you haven't spent time reading them before, you may find them to be fairly simple and straightforward.

That's what makes these words ones to struggle with. In a simple and straightforward way, they say things that are easy to understand. What isn't so easy to understand, though, is why the perfect Son of God would speak these words as he's murdered by sinful humans.

Luke 23:32-34—*Two other men, both criminals, were also led out with him to be executed. When they came to the place called the Skull, there they crucified him, along with the criminals—one on his right, the other on his left. Jesus said, "Father, forgive them, for they do not know what they are doing." And they divided up his clothes by casting lots.*

In his gospel, St. John records for us a particularly chilling moment. One week before Good Friday, Jesus arrived at Bethany, a city just outside of Jerusalem. He had been there many times before. Bethany was the hometown of three siblings who seemed to be particularly close to Jesus: Mary, Martha, and Lazarus. Earlier in his ministry, Jesus had raised Lazarus from the dead after an illness had claimed his life four days earlier.[45] When Jesus came to their town the week before Good Friday, the family invited him to be a guest of honor at a dinner party.

---

[44] Good Friday is the yearly Christian commemoration of Jesus' death on the cross. Many churches still observe the tradition of hearing the seven words of Christ—the seven recorded statements he made from the cross—read in a worship service on that day.

[45] See John 11:38ff.

Jerusalem and the nearby towns were filled with people who had come to celebrate the Passover. The people soon found out that Jesus was in Bethany. But John tells us that they weren't just excited to see Jesus, they were excited to see Lazarus—the man who had died and had come back to life. That's when John records the chilling sentence: "So the chief priests made plans to kill Lazarus as well."[46] The leaders of the church knew that Lazarus had died. They knew that four days later he was raised to life. They knew Jesus was the one who raised him. And instead of recognizing Jesus as God's Son, they came to a different conclusion: *Now we'll have to kill Lazarus too.*[47]

Yet Jesus said, "Father, forgive them, for they do not know what they are doing." How could he say that? Many of the people who orchestrated his death *did* know! Many of Jesus' miracles were undeniable and well-known. Was Jesus speaking just about the Roman soldiers who were following orders? Did he simply mean that the religious leaders didn't understand the full impact of their actions?

Both of those answers have been suggested over the years, but there's a third answer worth thinking about: This is how the gracious God so often deals with us. He doesn't treat us as our sins deserve. And thank God for that. His love covers over a multitude of sins. He doesn't desire the death of the wicked. He speaks tenderly, with words that desire our salvation. The people he looked at were still in their sins—there was no repentance, no turning to God—but Jesus had a prayer for his Father that revealed his deepest longing: He wanted those murderers to be forgiven.

But the real difficulty with these words isn't how Jesus could say that these people didn't know what they were doing. Have you ever been hurt? disappointed by those you love? betrayed? You know how impossible the thought of forgiving can seem at times. But when God's Son looked down at those who knowingly and ruthlessly arranged his death and those who drove the nails through his hands and feet, he wanted nothing more than their forgiveness.

---

[46] John 12:10.

[47] Many of the religious leaders of Jesus' day recognized that Jesus was no mere man, not even a false prophet, and this isn't the only evidence. John 3:2 records another leader saying that Jesus' miracles proved he was from God.

Sometimes people hurt us and don't repent. Sometimes their sins don't seem to bother them in the least. We can't pronounce forgiveness to them. Christ himself said that if someone does not repent, we dare not yet forgive them. But what do you see when you look at them? See what Jesus sees: See people who sin, people who hurt you and betray you, people who knowingly do the worst of the worst; long for their forgiveness as Jesus did.

> **Luke 23:38-43**—*There was a written notice above him, which read:* THIS IS THE KING OF THE JEWS. *One of the criminals who hung there hurled insults at him: "Aren't you the Christ? Save yourself and us!" But the other criminal rebuked him. "Don't you fear God," he said, "since you are under the same sentence? We are punished justly, for we are getting what our deeds deserve. But this man has done nothing wrong." Then he said, "Jesus, remember me when you come into your kingdom." Jesus answered him, "I tell you the truth, today you will be with me in paradise."*

The man's own words were enough to condemn him. We don't know what he did in his past; all we know is that he himself understood that he deserved to die for his sins. As we read the other gospel accounts of the crucifixion, it seems as though this dying man had even used some of his last breaths to mock Christ.[48] It would be understandable if Jesus hadn't answered him at all. It would seem more than gracious enough if Jesus had just put an end to the man's suffering. But those weren't enough for Christ. Before that day ended, this horrible criminal was standing in heaven with Jesus.

Sometimes it's hard to believe that Jesus would have us forgive others this way. Someone hurts us and they say they're sorry and that's it? We forgive that simply? In a word, *yes.* Sometimes that's hard to believe and do. But there's something that seems more impossible yet.

Anyone standing near those crosses who heard Jesus' words must have struggled to believe them. But those words couldn't have been more amazing to anyone than they were to the dying criminal. That's

---

[48] See Matthew 27:44 and Mark 15:32.

how guilt works. It's the tool the devil uses to try to convince us that no matter how much God loves the world and how freely he forgives others, *my sins* are too great for God to forgive. It can't be that simple for God to erase all my guilt.

"Jesus sinners does receive; oh, may all this saying ponder."[49] That's the only thing we can do. Go back to these words again and again. Maybe your guilt does seem too great. Maybe it's hard to believe that God really would forgive someone who has done what you have done. So take time—often—to stand at the foot of the cross and to listen to how Jesus forgives. Are you the worst of the worst? Then thank God for his promise: You'll stand with him in heaven too. Jesus will deliver on that promise.

John 19:25-27—*Near the cross of Jesus stood his mother, his mother's sister, Mary the wife of Clopas, and Mary Magdalene. When Jesus saw his mother there, and the disciple whom he loved standing nearby, he said to his mother, "Dear woman, here is your son," and to the disciple, "Here is your mother." From that time on, this disciple took her into his home.*

There's a chart that hangs on the wall of most hospital rooms. Next to the numbers 1 through 10, it shows ten different faces in increasing levels of suffering. A doctor or nurse will ask a patient to look at the chart and rate his or her suffering. Next to the number 1 is a smiley face—no suffering at all. Next to the number 10 is a face contorted with pain, sweating profusely. Underneath it are the words, "Worst pain possible." When you have that kind of pain, you can barely answer the doctor. In fact, you can barely process his or her question. When we have that kind of pain, it's all we can think about.

Pain does that to us in this life: it makes us think more about ourselves. It's natural for us to become inwardly focused. So much so, in fact, that we're often oblivious to the suffering that other people face. We are self-centered creatures. Pain just shows our real nature.

It shows God's real nature too. Jesus had gone without sleep. He had been subject to beatings and floggings. He had lost a staggering

---
[49] *Christian Worship* 304:1.

Hard Sayings of Jesus

amount of blood and was enduring incomprehensible pain. And he thought about his mother. He wanted her to be taken care of.

Jesus' words from the cross, as he speaks of forgiveness and mercy, show us so much about what *love* really looks like. Don't speed past these words. Jesus' words here rightly make us ashamed because we so often fail to show this kind of selfless love. And Jesus' words here rightly fill us with comfort because this is the perfect love that Jesus has for us.

> **Matthew 27:45,46**—*From the sixth hour until the ninth hour darkness came over all the land. About the ninth hour Jesus cried out in a loud voice,* "Eloi, Eloi, lama sabachthani?"—*which means,* "My God, my God, why have you forsaken me?"

Car accidents. Leukemia. Child abuse. War. These are terrible things. And the suffering they bring is far worse than anything most of us can imagine. Sometimes the people who are suffering those things will even describe their experiences as "going through hell." But those things aren't hell. As terrible as they are, nothing on earth can be as bad as hell. Hell is the complete absence of God's love and care. No one living on earth has ever truly endured hell.

Except for Jesus as he hung on the cross. That's what he wanted us to understand as he cried out, "My God, my God, why have you forsaken me?" On the cross, God's beloved Son was completely forsaken by God himself. No love. No comfort. No care. No good thing. God abandoned himself to suffer an eternity of hell.

There are two mysteries here that we'll never fully understand. The first has to do with the nature of God's being. How could God abandon himself? Jesus had clearly spoken about his complete unity with the Father on many occasions.[50] If the Father and the Son exist in unity, how could one abandon the other? If hell is the absence of God's love, how could God himself suffer it? Those mysteries are bound up in Christ's incarnation. Since Jesus is fully God and fully man, he experienced things separately from his Father in a way that we can't comprehend.

---

[50] John 10:30.

But the other mystery is more difficult yet. Why would Jesus do this? Why would a loving God abandon his perfect Son for the sake of sinners? God gives us only one answer: love. It seems impossible to understand a love that would go so far and suffer so much. It seems impossible that God would do that for a sinner like me. But that's exactly what he promised. We can't imagine what it's like to face suffering like that. And because of Jesus, we never will face suffering like that.

> **John 19:28,29**—*Later, knowing that all was now completed, and so that the Scripture would be fulfilled, Jesus said, "I am thirsty." A jar of wine vinegar was there, so they soaked a sponge in it, put the sponge on a stalk of the hyssop plant, and lifted it to Jesus' lips.*

It seems like the smallest of details. Jesus was thirsty. He cried out for a drink.

It's not the *what* of this statement that's so difficult. It's the *why*. St. John tells us that Jesus spoke these words so that "the Scripture would be fulfilled." Like so much of his suffering and death, God had ordained this event ahead of time.[51]

That's why these words are hard to read, and that's how they give us a window into Christ's love for us and commitment to us. Jesus knew the suffering that was waiting for him on the cross. Old Testament scriptures like Psalm 22 and Isaiah chapter 53 painted vivid, clear, and horrible pictures of what the Messiah's suffering and death would be like. Long before the first Good Friday, Jesus knew about the beating, the flogging, the nails, even the thirst. And he went to it willingly. He did it "so that the Scripture would be fulfilled."

It's hard to understand that kind of love and commitment, but there is such great blessing in knowing it! Apart from Jesus, it's easy to think that God is distant and removed from us. He's an all-powerful

---

[51] There's some uncertainty about which Scripture Jesus is referring to here. A natural assumption would be Psalm 22. Many details of Jesus' crucifixion are predicted there in precise terms. Psalm 22 doesn't have a direct reference to Jesus' asking for a drink, though 22:15 does speak about his intense thirst on the cross. Another possible reference is Psalm 69:21, which refers to enemies giving a person gall and vinegar to drink.

spirit. What could he know about the suffering and pain of human existence? No wonder so many people have struggled with the question, "Where is God when it hurts?"

These words show us where. In Jesus, we see so clearly that God isn't far away from our pain. He doesn't ignore our pain. He runs to it. Knowing full well all that he would suffer, Jesus went to the cross to fulfill every last prophecy about the price he had to pay to deliver this world from hell. Where is God when it hurts? Right there with us, in the middle of the pain. Even more than that: Jesus came to suffer the worst pain and punishment for our sins so that we wouldn't have to.

> **John 19:30**—*When he had received the drink, Jesus said, "It is finished." With that, he bowed his head and gave up his spirit.*

Again, Jesus' words from the cross are easy to understand. With his suffering behind him, Jesus stated his victory: *"It is finished."* The Son of God had suffered all and was about to give up his life. His work was done. The sins of all people had been atoned for. Heaven stood open. The Greek word John used to record Jesus' statement can just as accurately be translated "paid in full." That's what Jesus did on the cross. He paid for our sins in full.

That's easy to understand. It's not always easy to believe. So John added one more piece of information to help us. When my last hour on earth comes, I'll die. I won't have a choice. At God's call, my spirit will leave my body and go to the God who gave it. That's something we have no control over; even though our sin is forgiven, its mortal consequence still comes to us all. But Jesus didn't simply die. He *"gave up his spirit."* When you struggle to believe that it really *is* finished, that your sins really have been paid in full, go back to these little words. Jesus' life wasn't taken from him; he'd already accomplished his goal. He was able to give it willingly. His work was done. Your sins are gone.

> **Luke 23:44-47**—*It was now about the sixth hour, and darkness came over the whole land until the ninth hour, for the sun stopped shining. And the curtain of the temple was torn in two. Jesus called out with a loud voice, "Father, into your hands I commit my spirit." When he had said this, he breathed his last. The centurion, seeing*

what had happened, praised God and said, "Surely this was a righteous man."

Here, finally, is the one statement from the cross that we don't need to struggle with at all. This is the way things ought to be! God's Son could express complete confidence in his Father's care. He wasn't forsaken or abandoned anymore. He knew that his Father loved him and would protect him.

The centurion standing by the cross watched a good man die. But something more than that happened. Humankind's substitute died. What took place on the cross took place for the sake of Adam and Eve, for Peter and the disciples, for that centurion, and for you and me. God's perfect Son, the one true righteous man, laid down his life in our place.

Everything that Jesus did and said on the cross was in our place. That's especially important to remember as we consider his last statement. Because Jesus had paid the price for every sin, he could die confident of God's love for him. Because Jesus paid the price for every sin, these are your words too. You can live and die confident of God's love for you.

Jesus' words from the cross aren't difficult to understand. They're difficult because they speak such unbelievable truths about how deep and wide God's love is. They're difficult because they go so contrary to the thoughts of our own hearts. Perhaps that's why Jesus spoke these statements with the most simple, straightforward words. They're difficult, but he doesn't want us to struggle with them. He wants us to believe them.

13 "So They Won't Hear"

John 3:16—*"God so loved the world that he gave his one and only Son, that whoever believes in him shall not perish but have eternal life."*

Matthew 11:28—*"Come to me, all you who are weary and burdened, and I will give you rest."*

John 11:25—*"I am the resurrection and the life. He who believes in me will live, even though he dies; and whoever lives and believes in me will never die."*

They called Jesus *teacher* during his earthly ministry. It's not hard to see why. Through these chapters, I pray you've seen that even in his difficult sayings, Jesus wants to share knowledge and life with us. Sometimes poor translations or traditions complicate that. Sometimes his words are hard because they don't seem true or they challenge our views of life and of ourselves, but Jesus is always there to teach. He wants us to understand the truths of God.

So why would he say he doesn't?

Jesus told his disciples a parable. In his beautiful and simple illustration, he spoke of a farmer scattering seeds everywhere he could. The seeds fell on different kinds of soils and produced different results. Some grew. Some didn't. After he told his parable,

Matthew 13:10-17—*The disciples came to him and asked, "Why do you speak to the people in parables?" He replied, "The knowledge of the secrets of the kingdom of heaven has been given to you, but not to them. Whoever has will be given more, and he will have an abundance. Whoever does not have, even what he has will be taken from him. This is why I speak to them in parables: Though seeing, they do not see; though hearing, they do not hear or understand. In them is fulfilled the prophecy of Isaiah: 'You will be ever hearing but never understanding; you will be ever seeing but never perceiving. For this people's heart has become calloused; they hardly hear with their ears, and they have closed their eyes. Otherwise they might see with their* *eyes, hear with their ears, understand with their hearts and turn, and I would heal them.' But blessed are your eyes because they see, and your ears because they hear. For I tell you the truth, many prophets and righteous men longed to see what you see but did not see it, and to hear what you hear but did not hear it."*

It's not the answer you'd expect. Parables are earthly stories with heavenly meanings. They're illustrations that are meant to use something simple and "known" to help people understand a spiritual truth that we might not otherwise recognize. They're intended to teach.

Except this time, Jesus seems to say they weren't. At least, not always and not for everyone. Jesus talks about taking away from people. He seems to say that his reason for speaking in parables is so that some people do not understand them.

Jesus quotes from chapter 6 of Isaiah. In that chapter, Isaiah records the day the Lord commissioned him to be a prophet. When Isaiah (eventually!) responds to God's call with joy and zeal, the Lord gives him a surprising mission:

Isaiah 6:9,10—*"Go and tell this people: 'Be ever hearing, but never understanding; be ever seeing, but never perceiving.' Make the heart of this people calloused; make their ears dull and close their eyes. Otherwise they might see with their eyes, hear with their ears, understand with their hearts, and turn and be healed."*

It's not that God didn't want them to be saved. If you doubt that, read Isaiah chapter 5. Under the heading "The Song of the Vineyard," we hear about God's great love for his people. He cared for them. He gave them every blessing. He sent them his prophets and blessed them with priests. He gave them everything! But they didn't return his love. They rejected his Word. They damned themselves.

But God didn't want their rejection to lead to the damnation of all people. That's why he says what he says in Isaiah chapter 6. After giving Isaiah his difficult commission, the Lord talked about the destruction he would bring on Israel. It would be like laying waste to a forest, with this result: "The holy seed will be the stump in the land."[52]

---

[52] Isaiah 6:13.

God sent Isaiah to harden the hearts of the Israelites. The people who repeatedly refused to repent would be confirmed in their wickedness, and God would destroy their land and lead them away as slaves. Why? Because he loved the world. He would not let the people of Judah continue to destroy and neglect his message, so he was going to crush and humble them. But the Word would remain. And 70 years after God brought this judgment on his people, a remnant would return and listen to his Word again. The promise of the Savior would not be lost. The people would remain there until the Christ was born. God brought judgment on some to preserve his Word for others.

God still sometimes does that through his Word today. The Lord "who wants all people to be saved and to come to a knowledge of the truth"[53] will sometimes use his Word to harden the hearts of people who reject or abuse his Word. A friend who refuses to hear God's call to repent may just get angrier every time you share what God says until he just views God as a controlling monster instead of a loving master. Some family members hear in every gospel promise of God an excuse to live however they want until they're convinced they have no need for God at all. And at times like that, the Lord can use his Word to harden their hearts in that sin so that his Word won't continue to be trampled. That's God's judgment on their sin. And in doing so, God seeks to uphold his Word for others.

Should we be scared that the Lord could do that to us? Absolutely! Read through Romans 11:17-24. Paul uses the same imagery of a vineyard that God once used through Isaiah. Even though God destroyed the vineyard of Judah, the gospel still remains. And God grafts us into Christ like wild branches attached to the vine. That's God's grace and love: he does want all people to be saved! But, Paul reminds us, we should take Judah's example to heart. Our spiritual life comes from hearing and believing God's Word. If we stop doing that, our connection to God is lost. He will break us off of the vine so that others might be saved.

---

[53] 1 Timothy 2:4 (NIV 2011).

"So They Won't Hear"

But even when God sends his Word to harden hearts, his goal is still the same: it's always to save people through the preaching and hearing of his Word. Listen for that as Jesus explains the point of his parable of the sower:

> **Matthew 13:18-23**—*"Listen then to what the parable of the sower means: When anyone hears the message about the kingdom and does not understand it, the evil one comes and snatches away what was sown in his heart. This is the seed sown along the path. The one who received the seed that fell on rocky places is the man who hears the word and at once receives it with joy. But since he has no root, he lasts only a short time. When trouble or persecution comes because of the word, he quickly falls away. The one who received the seed that fell among the thorns is the man who hears the word, but the worries of this life and the deceitfulness of wealth choke it, making it unfruitful. But the one who received the seed that fell on good soil is the man who hears the word and understands it. He produces a crop, yielding a hundred, sixty or thirty times what was sown."*

God wants all people to be saved. "Faith comes from hearing the message" of God's Word.[54] But when that Word is preached, it won't always have the same results. Jesus knows that. And we so often witness this as we share God's Word.

Don't conclude that the problem is with the Word! We want to see people come to faith and be saved too. When the Word is met with rejection, it's tempting to think that changing the words will solve the problem. Consider the "hard sayings" of Jesus we have looked at in these pages. Wouldn't it be better for the kingdom if we made them easier? Perhaps we could take out what he says about the cost of discipleship or delete his calls to love him more than our own families. Maybe if we preached it in just the right way, it would never harden anyone's heart and everyone would see and believe!

Christ himself tells us that isn't true. *Because* his message is so different than this world's way of thinking, *because* it points us to a free grace that we'd never imagine on our own, *because* it shows us a

---

[54]Romans 10:17.

God we need more than anything else in this life, *because* there is evil in our hearts, *because* we naturally put our trust in our money and goods, *because* holding to God's truths will always bring some earthly persecution and call for sacrifice, Jesus says that when the true gospel is preached, it will so often be rejected. It will sometimes be like seed that never truly takes root.

But keep preaching it, Jesus says. *Simply sow the seed.* Be like the farmer in Jesus' parable. Even though you know the seed won't always take root and grow, still scatter it as far and wide as you can. Let it fall on every heart, be heard by every ear, and be seen by every eye. When Jesus' hard—but wonderful!—truths are preached, some hearts will become more calloused, some ears will hardly hear, and some eyes will close. Some, but not all. "The one who received the seed that fell on good soil is the man who hears the word and understands it. He produces a crop, yielding a hundred, sixty or thirty times what was sown" (Matthew 13:23).

Praise be to God that his Word has done that in your heart.

Glory be to God as you share his truths with others.

Postscript

Which are the *hard sayings of Jesus?* Different believers would no doubt give you different answers. Some would think of his shocking statement to cut off one's hand if it causes you to sin. Perhaps a heartbroken young husband or betrayed friend would consider Jesus' hardest saying to be his call to forgive our brother or sister "up to seventy-seven times."

There's not one list of Jesus' hard sayings. Perhaps these chapters touched on the ones that you find most difficult or puzzling. Maybe you can think of some glaring omissions.

Regardless of which statements of Christ challenge you most, I leave you with two encouragements:

1. Everything Jesus says is meant to bring us back to his love. Remember that when his statements push you or challenge you—even when they anger you. Whether he's rebuking us for our sin or calling us to a difficult task in life, every last statement comes from the same heart that led Jesus to the cross for you.

2. Struggling with Jesus' hard statements brings great blessings. Working on this book reminded me of that again. So often some of his sayings are so very hard because they are exactly the opposite of how we think or what we want to hear. But that's why we need them. They force us to wrestle with what grace really is and with what it really means to know God as the true source of blessing and love in our lives. Jesus is using these statements to draw us closer to God's heart.

May God continue to bless your struggles.